LEWIS & CLARK
REFRAMED

LEWIS & CLARK
REFRAMED

EXAMINING TIES TO
COOK, VANCOUVER, AND MACKENZIE

DAVID L. NICANDRI

FOREWORD BY
CLAY S. JENKINSON

WSU
PRESS

Washington State University Press
Pullman, Washington

WSU PRESS
WASHINGTON STATE UNIVERSITY

Washington State University Press
PO Box 645910
Pullman, Washington 99164-5910
Phone: 800-354-7360
Email: wsupress@wsu.edu
Website: wsupress.wsu.edu

Library of Congress Cataloging-in-Publication Data

Names: Nicandri, David L., 1948- author. | Jenkinson, Clay, writer of foreword.
Title: Lewis and Clark reframed : examining ties to Cook, Vancouver, and
    Mackenzie / David L. Nicandri.
Other titles: Examining ties to Cook, Vancouver, and Mackenzie
Description: Pullman, Washington : WSU Press, Washington State University,
    [2020] | Includes bibliographical references and index.
Identifiers: LCCN 2020025625 | ISBN 9780874223804 (paperback)
Subjects: LCSH: Lewis and Clark Expedition (1804-1806) | Lewis, Meriwether,
    1774-1809. | Clark, William, 1770-1838. | Explorers--Northwest,
    Pacific--History--18th century. | Northwest, Pacific--Discovery and
    exploration--Historiography. | Cook, James, 1728-1779--Influence. |
    Vancouver, George, 1757-1798--Influence. | Mackenzie, Alexander,
    1764-1820--Influence. | Lewis, Meriwether, 1774-1809. Original journals
    of the Lewis and Clark expedition, 1804-1806.
Classification: LCC F592.7 .N435 2020 | DDC 917.804/2--dc23
LC record available at https://lccn.loc.gov/2020025625

On the cover: Image of George Vancouver from Wikimedia Commons.
Other images used courtesy of the Washington State Historical Society.
Design by Scott Swanger.

CONTENTS

To Clay Jenkinson,
My friend and fellow citizen in the
Republic of Letters

FOREWORD:
THE ROAD TO GRINDER'S STAND

In my opinion, David Nicandri is now the freshest and most interesting voice in Lewis and Clark scholarship.[1] *Lewis and Clark Reframed: Examining Ties to Cook, Vancouver, and Mackenzie* is his second book on the Lewis and Clark Expedition. His previous volume, *River of Promise: Lewis and Clark on the Columbia* (2009), filled an interpretive vacuum. Few previous books had given the Pacific slope travels of Lewis and Clark the attention they deserve. Thanks to Nicandri's extraordinary work of scholarship, all subsequent studies of Lewis and Clark in the Columbia basin must now begin with a mastery of his analysis and reflections. *River of Promise* also challenged some of the received traditions of the expedition, particularly the myth that Lewis and Clark were such congenial friends that they never experienced a moment of tension out there, and the idea that the Shoshone-Hidatsa woman Sacagawea was the most important Native American they met in their twenty-eight months of travel.

Nicandri, formerly the director of the Washington State Historical Society and more recently the author of a study of Captain James Cook's third and final voyage, is not content to retell the Lewis and Clark story in his own inimitable prose. He seeks to break new ground, to increase the number of lenses through which we view the expedition, and to engage the journals as literary texts, not merely as a data mine from which to construct yet another tidy narrative about the most famous journey of exploration in American history. As he put it in a recent interview, Nicandri's goal when he writes about Lewis and Clark is not to get into their shoes (or, as Clark would say, *mockersons*), but into their heads.

During the bicentennial of the Lewis and Clark Expedition (2003–2006), one prominent historian declared that the subject was essentially exhausted. We can keep retelling the story again and again, he said, but there is really nothing more to say. In my view, he could not have been more wrong. First and foremost, the publication of the University of Nebraska edition of *The Journals of the Lewis & Clark Expedition* (1983–2001) was not the end but a new beginning. Thanks to the painstaking work of Dr. Gary Moulton and his editorial advisers, we finally have a comprehensive standard gathering of all the known journals of the expedition under one multi-volume roof, employing settled and consistent editing protocols, superbly annotated. Before that signature event in the history of the expedition's journals, scholars found themselves drawing their material from disparate sources often bearing the marks of different editorial procedures. The best previous comprehensive edition of the journals was out of print. A scholar could never be sure she or he had access to everything necessary to draw conclusions, and quotations from the "journals" were couched in several inconsistent editorial conventions. Moulton's achievement is an invitation for everyone who finds this story compelling to read through the whole documentary record with fresh eyes. That is precisely what David Nicandri has done.

Perhaps more to the point, every generation has to reinterpret Lewis and Clark, just as we reinterpret Shakespeare, Dante, George Eliot, Cicero, Jane Austen, Herodotus, and Emily Dickinson. One need only read through the books of previous generations of even the best Lewis and Clark scholars to see how much has changed. Attitudes toward Native Americans, women, the Europeanization of the North American continent, the character and vision of Thomas Jefferson, and the natural world have undergone a dramatic metamorphosis since Bernard DeVoto published his concise edition of the journals in 1953. Compare DeVoto's groundbreaking *Journals of Lewis and Clark* with Frank Bergon's 1989 selection by the same name. In DeVoto we have a geopolitical adventure story in the history of exploration, with the fewest possible journal entries about the flora and fauna of the expedition. Bergon is so dedicated to the natural history of the expedition that his edition sometimes becomes tedious as a narrative of the journey. It is not possible to read some of the previous Lewis and Clark books without cringing over some offhand comments, phrases, and lines of argument that would now be regarded as insufficiently generous or culturally insensitive. This is not to criticize those important works of scholarship. It is indisputable, however, that we now have a fuller, richer, more nuanced, and more generous understanding of the story, particularly with respect to the role of Native Americans in the expedition.

Until the 1980s and 1990s, the expedition was almost inevitably seen as a journey of good will and innocence. Lewis and Clark came in peace for all mankind, sought neither to purchase land nor displace Indians, and if they cracked open cultures that could only maintain their traditional life-way by being left "undiscovered," members of the Corps of Discovery were unaware that they had disturbed things forever for those indigenous peoples. Besides, those twentieth century historians thought, if not Lewis and Clark, some other Anglo-Europeans would certainly have lifted the veil on the American indigenous Arcadia. Nothing is more tenacious in discussions of the history of the American West than the "myth of inevitability"—that what happened to Native Americans between 1492 and December 29, 1890 (Wounded Knee), was a sad but unavoidable destiny. Until recently, Lewis and Clark were exempted from the idea that beginning with the Revolution and the Northwest Ordinance of 1787, the United States had engaged in a systematic dispossession of American Indians. If this was not quite a policy of genocide, then certainly it represented a tragic imposition of attempted cultural genocide. In the "old history," Native Americans were relegated to the status of bit players (or the romanticized Sacagawea) on a stage dominated by the thirty-three members of the permanent party, particularly the two captains, John Colter, York, George Shannon, George Drouillard, and John Shields. Narratives of the expedition were cheerfully triumphalist in tone. Meriwether Lewis and William Clark were seen as virtual doppelgangers, with Lewis perhaps regarded as better educated and somewhat more prone to melancholia. And "Sacajawea" the guide.

That was then. On this side of that cultural continental divide, the two captains are increasingly seen as quite—often dramatically—distinct individuals who shared the same trip but not quite the same journey, until it is now sometimes possible to wonder how they got along so harmoniously given their very different ways of seeing the world. The triumphalism of previous generations has wiped its smile off its face. Today the expedition occupies a more problematic place in the history of the nineteenth century. The story is now one of adventure but also loss—loss to the more than fifty Native American tribes Lewis and Clark met along the way, loss to the pristine wilderness of pre-Enlightenment and preindustrial America, loss of species, loss of habitat, loss of the great pre-dam, free-flowing rivers beyond the Appalachian Mountains, but also the loss of what historian William Goetzmann called the west of the imagination, inhabited for Jefferson with mountains of salt, mammoths and mastodons, symmetrical mountain ranges, and a geo-utopian "height of land" from which all the waters flowed to various seas.

The watershed moment in modern Lewis and Clark studies came in 1984 with the publication of James Ronda's seminal *Lewis and Clark among the Indians*. Ronda's ingenious prestidigitation—reverse the lens and look at the expedition through the eyes of Native Americans for a change—immediately opened whole new worlds of interpretive possibility, still not fully explored by subsequent scholars and Native American historians. We now have a *Lewis and Clark among the Nez Perce* (Allen V. Pinkham and Steven R. Evans, 2013), but we need Lewis and Clark among the Mandan, among the Lakota, among the Blackfeet, among the Shoshone, among the Clatsop, among the Arikara, among the Osage, and more. Ronda's book remains the foundation of all future Lewis and Clark studies, but he wrote it almost forty years ago. Ronda himself acknowledges that it is time for a new, fuller synthesis along the lines of *Lewis and Clark among the Indians*, taking advantage of all the archaeology, environmental studies, Native American oral histories, and publications about Indians *by* Indians that came after his ground-breaking treatment of the subject.

In fact, the two most influential modern books about Lewis and Clark, Ronda's 1984 study and Stephen Ambrose's *Undaunted Courage: Meriwether Lewis, Thomas Jefferson, and the Opening of the American West* (1996), have accomplished their missions so successfully that they now need to be updated to take advantage of all that we have learned in the last twenty-five years. In addition to that, Ronda has endorsed the view that more rehashings of the baseline narrative will not take Lewis and Clark studies to the next level. In his last major public lecture on the expedition, he urged scholars, authors, amateur historians, and lovers of the trail to get out of the river and over the bluffs, to begin to elucidate the Lewis and Clark Expedition by way of other exploration literature, by consulting a wider historical and literary context, by using the new tools of cultural studies and postmodernism to look at the expedition journals in a fresh way, and by asking ourselves what we think we know about the expedition and why we think we know it. Nobody has taken Professor Ronda's challenge more seriously than David Nicandri.

Nicandri is precisely the right person to navigate these new interpretive waters. He knows and loves the story. He has no ax to grind. His response to the perplexities, textual mysteries and oddities, and to the unresolved tensions of the journals is as playful as it is earnest, and while he debunks some of our too-long untested mythologies about the expedition, he does so with clarity, charity, and bemusement. He is not afraid to speculate, but in every one of those moments, he grounds his speculation in plausible evidence. Among other things, it just a pleasure to read Nicandri's prose—incisive, learned, often witty, with a vocabulary that makes one smile, not grimace, as one reaches for the dictionary.

After all, after more than a century of hectic Lewis and Clark scholarship—some of it as particular as identifying the site of Fort Clatsop or Dismal Nitch, some of it as lofty as attempting to determine what President Jefferson regarded as the long term fate of American Indians—a startling number of mysteries abide: what happened to Lewis's dog Seaman? What exactly did Sacagawea contribute to the success of the expedition? How long did she live? And where did she die? Why did Lewis never write his book(s)? How, exactly, did Lewis die on the night of October 11, 1809? If he was murdered, who, how, and why? If he committed suicide, how exactly do the forensics line up with the known facts of the case? And of course, why would Meriwether Lewis kill himself? Where is the iron boat? What happened to Fort Mandan? How much DNA did the expedition leave behind along the trail? What precisely were the social dynamics of a permanent party of thirty-three traversing the continent at close quarters for more than two years? It is surprising how little is actually known about these mysteries. Our assessment of the Lewis and Clark story will never end. It is at least possible that previously unnoticed documents will surface, including perhaps the "lost journals" of Frazer and others, the rumored private diary of Lewis, more letters, War Department documents, previously undiscovered letters, and more. Meanwhile, the journals as Professor Moulton has gathered them need to be read with fresh eyes, day by day, often line by line.

In his previous book, *River of Promise: Lewis and Clark on the Columbia*, Nicandri bravely took on some of these questions. Among other things, he attempted to determine what part of Lewis's post expedition disintegration was related to the events of the expedition, particularly during the under-studied return journey of March to September 1806. It was Nicandri who suggested that Lewis—emotionally and spiritually exhausted, increasingly impatient with the ways of indigenous people, and homesick—suffered from a kind of slow-motion nervous breakdown on the return journey. He revisits Lewis's homesickness at Fort Clatsop in one of the most thoughtful essays in this volume. He also attempted to reset our understanding of one of the most famous Indian women of American history, Sacagawea. His argument was simple, if to some exasperating: if you remove your fantasy lens and romantic spectacles, it becomes clear that Sacagawea has, at the very least, been overrated as the expedition's guide and as a good-will ambassador in the Columbia basin. In fact, Nicandri suggested that our fixation on Sacagawea has blinded us to the more important guiding and diplomatic contributions made by other Native Americans, particularly Tetoharsky and Twisted Hair of the Nez Perce, who voluntarily took on the role as "conductors" of the expedition as it moved west of what is now Idaho into the lower Columbia. Nicandri also insisted that Lewis took advantage of his partner in discovery William Clark in several ways, first by finding reasons to get out ahead of the exploring party when he sensed a big moment of discovery just over the horizon, but also in appropriating key geographic information about the Rocky Mountains that indisputably came from an earlier reconnaissance led by Clark. Finally, Nicandri almost singlehandedly rescued Joseph Whitehouse from obscurity and proved that the usually neglected private—in part because he was *not* an officer—frequently recorded information in his journal that escaped the notice of the captains and sergeants or did not seem to merit their attention.

Nicandri has always had a special interest in the journal of Private Joseph Whitehouse, now one of the treasures of the Newberry Library in Chicago. In one of the more memorable passages in this book, Nicandri shows that Whitehouse lifted the preface of his journal directly from Alexander Mackenzie's *Voyages from Montreal*, changing only the name of the nation most likely to benefit from his travels. Where Mackenzie had spoken of the advantages of the fur trade to the British dominions, Whitehouse spoke of the region through which he traveled as now "a part belonging to the United states."

If it is true that Lewis found ways to make sure that he was what Nicandri calls "the solitary hero" at the big discovery moments of the expedition, we may feel a touch of indignation on behalf of William Clark, whose contribution to the success of the expedition we now regard as at least equal to that of his commanding officer, but as lovers of the literature of exploration we have reason to be glad that Lewis got his way. Lewis's journal entries for June 13, 1805, when he reached the Great Falls, for August 12, when he first drank from the source of the "mighty & heretofore deemed endless Missouri," and particularly for one day earlier, August 11, 1805, when Lewis made contact with the elusive and timid Shoshone, are spectacular performances in exploration prose. Whenever Clark and Lewis both write about one of the sublime moments of the expedition—such as the departure from Fort Mandan on April 7, 1805—Lewis is eloquent, sometimes grandiloquent, while Clark is factual, descriptive, straight forward—in short, prosaic. The journals of Lewis and Clark would be comparatively impoverished had Clark commanded alone. Just imagine for a moment a Clark entry on the first encounter with Cameahwait and the Shoshone. It would have been competent and reliable, of course, but there would have been no drama, no irony, no use of the word "metamorphosed," and we certainly would not have been entertained with Lewis's snarky reaction to the "national hug." As Thomas Slaughter argued in *Exploring Lewis and Clark: Reflections on Men and Wilderness* (2003), a provocative rereading of the expedition that has influenced the work of several subsequent historians, including Nicandri, it is one thing to explore, but it is what the explorer later writes about the journey that establishes his place in the history of exploration. However much it wounds those who prefer Clark to Lewis to acknowledge, without Lewis's literary genius the expedition's journals would be dramatically less compelling and the place of the expedition in American memory would be diminished.

It may be thought that academic postmodernism operates at a far remove from the historical journals of Lewis and Clark, but in fact it offers useful tools and perspectives with which to readdress a story we thought we knew inside and out. Thanks to the cultural studies movement—structuralism, deconstruction, gender studies, historicism, postmodernism—we have learned to be especially skeptical about taking any text, any phrase even, at face value. We are reminded that the journals of Lewis and Clark are as significant for what they omit as for what they articulate. We are now invited to scrutinize the journals as texts rather than as a straightforward linear narrative. We are encouraged to "place" the journals not merely in the context of Enlightenment travel and Thomas Jefferson's America, but in the still larger context of the history of exploration, dating back at least to Captain James Cook and—arguably—earlier. Nor are we any longer confined to read the journals as history. As Nicandri reminds us several times in this book, the journals must be seen as belonging to a literary tradition, not merely hearkening back to previous travel journals and expedition reports, but belonging, too, to the seemingly unrelated literary and cultural tradition of Britain, the United States, and the European continent, particularly France. As Nicandri admirably shows, even the seemingly rudimentary and prosaic field journal accounts of an explorer of such literary modesty as William Clark have their echoes in a broader literary tradition.

Moreover, Nicandri is as alive to the literature of the Enlightenment and the eighteenth century as he is to the protocols of exploration. Like the late Joe Mussulman, Nicandri is never content to shrug off the quirks, linguistic oddities, buried references and allusions, and unusual moments of diction, in the expedition journals. Thanks to his wide knowledge of the Anglo-American literature of the era, Nicandri is able to make the textual connections that not only illuminate his work but enable us to understand such previously perplexing words and phrases in the journals as "sublunary" and "indolent" (August 18, 1805), "darling project" (April 7, 1805), and "the pencil of Salvator Rosa" and the "pen of Thompson" [sic] (June 13, 1805). If Nicandri is not the first Lewis and Clark scholar to view the journals through the lens of the Scottish poet James Thomson's "The Seasons," he is the first since Albert Furtwangler's *Visions of America in the Lewis and Clark Journals* (1993). Given enough time, Nicandri is precisely the right person to produce a Lewis version of *The Road to Xanadu: A Study in the Ways of the Imagination,* John Livingston Lowes's 1927 classic study of the mental formation of the Romantic poet Samuel Taylor Coleridge. It could be called *The Road to Grinder's Stand.* Indeed, the question of Lewis's "education" (broadly defined) is the single greatest mystery of the Lewis biography. What had he read before he went to work for President Jefferson? What did he read in the library (now the state dining room) of Jefferson's White House between 1801 and 1803? What did he read at Monticello during Congressional recesses? And what did he read in Philadelphia in 1803 when Jefferson sent him to take a short course in Enlightenment science from such luminaries as Benjamin Smith Barton and Robert Patterson? If we had such a study—assuming that these matters could be teased out of primary and secondary sources and comparative curricula of the era—we would, I believe, be able to ground much more of what Lewis wrote in the context of allusion, reference, and literary borrowing.

Nicandri's eye for the telling detail makes him unique among Lewis and Clark scholars. Thus in Chapter 6 of *Lewis and Clark Reframed,* "Meriwether Lewis: The Solitary Hero," he spends a good deal of time exploring the key moment in August 1805 when Clark's abscessed feet prevented him from making first contact with the Shoshone. Lewis had been somewhat reluctantly willing to let Clark have his moment in the sun, but thanks to this unexpected turn of events (a lowly foot infection), Lewis now surged out of camp triumphantly to make the historic first encounter with the Shoshone. This led to one of Clark's few expressions of frustration, implicitly grousing about Lewis's insistence on always being first: "I Should have taken this trip had I been able to march." Nicandri rightly gives that loaded sentence the attention it deserves, but he caps his argument by quoting a much briefer but equally telling phrase from the journal of John Ordway: Lewis had gone ahead "to make discoveries." Precisely. Everyone understood the dynamics of exploration. Clark moved the boats, Lewis made discoveries.

Nobody can fulfill Ronda's cross-cultural challenge fully, but Nicandri has an advantage over most other Lewis and Clark scholars—he is deeply grounded in the travels of Captain James Cook, whose exploration style and protocols became the foundation for all that followed; and he knows, too, the travels of Alexander Mackenzie, who had an even more immediate influence on Lewis and especially Clark. A good example of Nicandri's application of the Cook protocol is his attempt to identify the Lewis and Clark Expedition's journal keepers for whom we do not have an extant journal or book. He tentatively identifies the "missing journal keepers" as Thomas Howard and John Potts from evidence in the captain's journals of the Great Falls to Three Forks segment of the expedition, and from the tradition of naming discoveries in other exploration narratives, particularly those of James Cook. We may disagree with Nicandri's conclusion, but it is a welcome improvement over the "it must have been X because he seems like the kind of guy who would keep a journal" approach of much previous Lewis and Clark discourse. This allows Nicandri to see the expedition through several lenses at once, a form of intellectual triangulation that pays dividends of great insight in his reading of Lewis and Clark.

By eschewing a broad linear narrative (the stuff of Ambrose's *Undaunted Courage*), and by paying very close attention to key phrases and strange locutions, Nicandri calls our attention to incidents, dynamics, and impressions that we tend to overlook in a plot-centered account of the journey. It is clear in all that he writes that Nicandri has done the hard reading. He knows the Lewis and Clark literature from Biddle to Patricia Tyson Stroud. His erudition and wide familiarity with things outside the usual boundaries of the Lewis and Clark story have enabled him to solve some of the remaining mysteries that lurk in the documentary record. Who previously knew that Mackenzie's *Voyages from Montreal* served "as a veritable trail guide" for Lewis and Clark or that the captains "emulated, and even plagiarized" many passages from Mackenzie's 1801 account? This argument was adumbrated in *River of Promise*; it gets a much more thorough examination here.

To the received wisdom that Lewis never prepared a single line for the publication of his report, Nicandri argues that many of Lewis's journal entries are not daily field notes, but literary compositions based on real or remembered field notes and experiences. And that Lewis did write a lengthy treatise for his book, an "Essay on Indian Policy," which Nicholas Biddle appended to his 1814 paraphrase edition of the expedition's travels. My own view is that much of what we like to think of as Lewis's "journal" of 1805–06 was written or extensively rewritten in Philadelphia in 1807, that Lewis was using the collections of the American Philosophical Society and the Library Company of Philadelphia to dress up his narrative and to turn essentially pedestrian field notes (not always his own) into the literary prose of exploration. It was there, I think, that Lewis was most likely to read the poetry of James Thomson and the reports of Captain Cook. Nicandri and I never get together without wrestling with what might be called "the dynamics of the journals," especially Lewis's, for hours at a time. I heartily agree with his view that "Lewis's westering journal was not a field diary written each night around the campfire, but was instead a retrospective second-generation reflection probably intended as the first draft of a book he never got around to publishing."

If this remarkable book were remembered for nothing else, Nicandri will be credited with calling attention to the life and achievement of Mahlon Dickerson (1770–1853), U.S. Senator, Governor of New Jersey, Secretary of the Navy, and perhaps the best friend Meriwether Lewis ever had. In most studies of Lewis and Clark, Dickerson is portrayed as a drinking pal and confidant of Lewis in the "lost year" (1807–08), when Lewis was ostensibly writing his account of the expedition and working in Philadelphia with printers, scientists, and illustrators to get his three-volume report into print before venturing to St. Louis to take up his duties as territorial governor. Nicandri follows up Donald Jackson's lead in connecting Dickerson first to Lewis (after and *before* the 1803–06 expedition), then to Charles Wilkes' scientific circumnavigation of the world (1838–42), and finally (and less emphatically) to the western travels of John C. Frémont. One gets the sense that for all of the shared adventure of William Clark and Meriwether Lewis, their friendship had more to do with a shared mission, an unapparelled and perilous adventure, and a shared set of values about the future of the American West, than with the workings of the heart. It had a number of elements, but it was primarily a professional friendship. With Dickerson, Lewis—lonely, vaguely lovelorn or posing as such, at least in his own mind inadequate to the task of finishing his book, and quite possibly suffering from a kind of post-expedition PTSD—was apparently able to find an emotional intimacy that he certainly could not have with his mentor and patron Jefferson (that intensely private stoic on the mountain), and probably not with the more stable and affable Clark either. At any rate, long after Lewis's suicide Dickerson called Lewis "the most sincere friend I ever had." Their nocturnal wanderings in the suburbs and outskirts of Philadelphia in 1807 have a lovely melancholic ring to them, two bachelors wandering the margins of the cultural capital of the United States, perplexed by their inability (or perhaps unwillingness) to settle into the middle stream of their lives. If we could know more about any single relationship of Lewis's life, I believe it would be the nature of his conversations with Dickerson when they were not, pro forma, discussing the "girls of Philadelphia." Among other things, one would give anything to know how Lewis talked about Thomas Jefferson with a trusted friend. Nicandri's excellent scholarship and the careful and appreciative way he writes about the Dickerson–Lewis friendship is one of his best contributions to Lewis and Clark studies.

In the epilogue of *Lewis and Clark Reframed*, Nicandri's insightful survey of where things now stand in Lewis and Clark studies, he writes, "perhaps the greatest contribution Lewis and Clark scholars can [hereafter] make is a full-fledged delineation of the expedition within its Enlightenment roots." I could not agree more. And in fact, Nicandri's book is the first serious pass at what Dave, with his usual flare for diction, might call "that great desideratum."

Clay S. Jenkinson
May 2020

 NOTES

1. When I wrote this foreword, I did not know that David Nicandri was dedicating this book to me or that he had written so generously about me in his acknowledgments. Had I known, I might have declined his invitation. I wrote this foreword merely because I greatly admire his work.

PREFACE

Writing on the eve of the bicentennial earlier this century, James P. Ronda called for new approaches to the study of Lewis and Clark. He believed that the expedition's story had been rounded into too familiar a form, preventing "fresh readings" that might break open or encourage new interpretive angles. Ronda pointed out that although Lewis and Clark were fixtures in the history of the American West "they have yet to be put in the wider context" of Enlightenment-era exploration. Clay Jenkinson summarized the potential of such an approach by observing that "new close readings of the journals" would result in a "liberation from the conventional (and largely mythic) national master narrative that has been permitted to pass for real history for so long."[1]

This book has been inspired by the critical insights of Ronda and Jenkinson, as was my previous study of the expedition, *River of Promise: Lewis and Clark on the Columbia*.[2] That volume was a more comprehensive study, emphasizing the course of exploration west of the Continental Divide, including the role that Native Americans, as cultural guides and topographic strategists, played in its success. In this more targeted analysis, I have attempted to find connections between the journals of these American captains and the published accounts of their approximate contemporaries: James Cook, George Vancouver, and Alexander Mackenzie, all of whom advanced the work of Pacific Northwest discovery for Great Britain.

Other Spanish, French, and both British and American fur trade expeditions reached the Pacific Northwest before Lewis and Clark, and in the last category the exploits of both John Meares and Robert Gray will be treated here in some detail. But the focus will remain on Cook, Vancouver, and Mackenzie because of their direct and at times hidden (or indirect) influence on the geographic outlook and literary tactics of Lewis and Clark once they reached the Pacific Slope. Meares and Gray followed Cook's track to the Northwest Coast after the latter's third and final voyage highlighted the potential for the maritime fur trade in sea otter pelts. But the limited, and frequently erroneous, geographic information gleaned from these fur men was later subsumed, and to an extent controverted by, what Vancouver and Mackenzie said about the region. Indeed, it was their accounts that Lewis and Clark studied and carried with them on their trek.

Assuredly, an extensive history of Lewis and Clark within the multinational, multidecadal, and multimodal quest for the Northwest Passage remains to be written. My aim is to help lay the groundwork for that future study. More specifically, I want to show how the American expedition, and its leaders' recording of it, was influenced by the preceding ventures of explorers who were furthering British interests. This is important because there is a tendency within the study of Lewis and Clark to view that enterprise as if it had entered a *tabula rasa*.

Characteristically, given the privileging of their time in the Missouri River Basin by scholars of the expedition, we already have in hand a partial corrective in W. Raymond Wood's *Prologue to Lewis and Clark: The Mackay and Evans Expedition.*[3] As documented by Wood, when Lewis and Clark reached St. Louis below the confluence of the Missouri and Mississippi Rivers in the fall of 1803, they entered a geographic zone that was well charted, even if it still qualified as the frontier of European-American settlement and engagement with a vibrant aboriginal population. The signal accomplishment in this regard was the 1795–97 expedition of James Mackay and John Evans. These men were British nationals enlisted by Spanish colonial officials to stave off Great Britain's incursions into the upper Missouri near the Mandan villages in present-day North Dakota. The premise behind the Mackay/Evans venture was that if Britain's fur trade expansion was left unaddressed, Spanish sovereignty over the entire Missouri River Basin was jeopardized.

Mackay, the nominal leader of this undertaking, only made it as far as the modern state of Nebraska. Evans continued on, with the intention of reaching the headwaters of the Missouri, if not the Pacific shore, but his trek too was cut short. He turned for home at the Mandan villages, having mapped the entire course of the river to that point from St. Louis. But by reaching that far, a full decade before Lewis and Clark, Evans was also able to access indigenous knowledge of western topography covering almost the whole width of Montana. This included features in Montana later denominated by the captains as the Great Falls of the Missouri and the Gates of the Mountains. Evans was likewise adept at securing some hints about the country west of the Continental Divide, such as the steep fall of water on the Great River of the West that drained the Pacific Slope, a watercourse named Columbia in 1792 by Robert Gray after his ship, *Columbia Rediviva.*

Lewis and Clark came into possession of a set of Evans's maps and a copy of his notes in St. Louis. Their journals for the upriver segment in 1804 are replete with references to this record. Ronda wrote in the foreword to Wood's book that the latter provided a glimpse into "the kind of world Lewis and Clark found when they voyaged up the river in 1804."[4] Indeed, the fact that Spanish, French, and British fur trade explorers over the last quarter of the eighteenth century had secured and disseminated detailed knowledge about the Missouri River from St. Louis to Mandan country goes a long way toward explaining the muted nature of Meriwether Lewis's journal for the first year of exploration. It is not unreasonable to assume that the same factor rationalizes Lewis's corresponding silence once the expedition reached the zone of discovery previously charted by Cook, Vancouver, and Mackenzie, this book's nexus.

Lewis and Clark Reframed is therefore an attempt to replicate the interpretive value of Wood's study with a parallel examination of the explorers who visited the Pacific Northwest before the captains. More particularly still, this book strives to describe the dynamics of exploratory journal construction. The work of discovery, unquestionably, involves the transmission of geographic comprehension through time and from explorer to explorer, but to an extent that is too little appreciated, exploration was also a literary phenomenon, and that is one of the major themes tying several chapters together.

The Lewis and Clark Expedition (to be sure, exploration history more generally) is a subject with enduring scholarly and popular interest and this book aims to appeal to both audiences. But there now exists, after the wave of publications that crested during the bicentennial and its immediate aftermath more than a decade ago, a dearth of new scholarly material about the expedition. This effort attempts to help fill the current vacuum, with a novel interpretive frame besides. By drawing serially on the extensive documentary compilations of John C. Beaglehole (Cook), W. Kaye Lamb (Vancouver and Mackenzie), and Gary E. Moulton (Lewis and Clark), this book is the first to extensively feature the work of these distinguished editors in a single volume. This approach breaks new ground by putting Lewis and Clark's expedition in a global context.

Several chapters are based on articles previously published in *Pacific Northwest Quarterly* and *We Proceeded On*, the journal of the Lewis and Clark Trail Heritage Foundation (see credits section for the full citations). I have juxtaposed revised versions of these essays with entirely new material, thereby creating a more accessible cross-expeditionary comparative analysis along the lines Ronda originally envisioned. The following reader's guide details my analytical journey, chapter by chapter.

Chapter 1, "Lewis and Clark in the Age of Cook," takes the widest perspective by describing Cook's role as the emblematic Enlightenment explorer and the first of several travelers to look for one or another of the cartographic variations on the Pacific Slope's gateway to the Northwest Passage.

Chapter 2, "Exploring under the Influence of Alexander Mackenzie," shows how Lewis and Clark used the Scotsman's preceding account, *Voyages from Montreal* (1801), as a virtual trail guide. The captains borrowed many field techniques and some of their favorite expressions from the North West Company fur trade explorer; indeed, they plagiarized entire paragraphs from that work.

Chapter 3, "The Rhyme of the Great Navigator: The Literature of Captain Cook and Its Influences on the Journals of Lewis and Clark," takes a more granular look at Cook's influence on the captains. A textual analysis shows that not only had Lewis and Clark relied heavily on Mackenzie, but so too on Cook. I focus on Lewis's specific reference to Cook when departing Fort Mandan; Clark's discussion of a (supposed) mistake Cook made in his description of Native canoe decoration; and how Lewis's most famous passage, written in awe of the Great Falls of the Missouri, was inspired by what he had read in the literature of Cook. I also suggest that Lewis's poignant birthday meditation of August 1805 was heavily influenced by literary sources he first became familiar with by reading the accounts of Captain Cook.

Chapter 4, "The Missing Journals: Some Clues on the Upper Missouri," explores one of the mysteries of the Lewis and Clark expedition—the identity of the two or three journal keepers whose records are now missing. Drawing on parallels in the Cook journals, I extrapolate from the captains' pattern on place naming to establish who the unknown scribes were.

Chapter 5, "The Illusion of Cape Disappointment," addresses one of the most controversial episodes in Lewis and Clark history. Approaching the Pacific Ocean, Clark famously exclaimed *"Ocian in view!"* The question has long raged about what Clark actually saw from his vantage point on the lower Columbia near Pillar Rock. I argue that he was heavily influenced in his expectations about what to expect when the expedition approached its goal at the Pacific by Vancouver's expeditionary narrative and cartography.

Chapter 6, "Meriwether Lewis: The Solitary Hero," shows that despite expedition lore positing that the captains were equals, Lewis claimed all the epochal moments of discovery for himself, and in one of his more memorable passages he drew on Mackenzie for inspiration.

Chapter 7, "Pure Water: Lewis's Homesickness at Fort Clatsop," draws on a key insight from the chief naturalist on Captain Cook's first voyage, Joseph Banks, who noticed the psychological effects that plagued the crew when the expedition's discovery phase came to an end. Banks called this phenomenon "nostalgia," a term that then held far more serious medical connotations than the modern usage associated with a fondness for "the good old days." Borrowing from parallels in Cook's and other exploratory accounts, we will see that Lewis, like many long-distance voyagers, was afflicted with this syndrome.

Chapter 8, "Lewis's 'dear friend' Mahlon Dickerson and the Fate of Early Nineteenth-Century American Exploration," analyzes Lewis's relationship with the man who, apart from Clark, was his best friend. The two met at Jefferson's table and then socialized together extensively in Philadelphia both before and after the expedition. Their relationship offers insights into Lewis's shortcomings and eventual undoing. However, in a rather unusual twist of fate (and one never remarked upon in the vast literature of Lewis and Clark), decades later Dickerson was the secretary of the navy under Presidents Jackson and Van Buren. In this capacity, he played a pivotal role in the development of the United States Exploring Expedition (1838–42), modeled in many respects after the template Cook made conventional half a century earlier. Dickerson also gave John C. Frémont, the first army explorer to track a portion of Lewis and Clark's trail in the Columbia Basin, his start in the work of discovery.

An epilogue, "Whither the Exploration of Lewis and Clark: Recent Trends and Future Directions," offers some reflections on several larger and interrelated themes that constitute future opportunities for the further contextualization of the Lewis and Clark story and the Enlightenment era of which it is a part.

──────── NOTES ────────

1. James P. Ronda, "Troubled Passages: The Uncertain Journeys of Lewis and Clark," *Oregon Historical Quarterly* 106: 4 (Winter 2005): 539; Ronda; "'The Writingest Explorers': The Lewis and Clark Expedition in American Historical Literature," in *Voyages of Discovery: Essays on the Lewis and Clark Expedition* (Helena: Montana Historical Society Press, 1998), 322; Clay Jenkinson, "Thomas Slaughter's Expedition: Exploring (and Deploring) Lewis and Clark," *Oregon Historical Quarterly* 105: 4 (Winter 2004): 631.
2. David L. Nicandri, *River of Promise: Lewis and Clark on the Columbia* (Bismarck, ND: Dakota Institute Press, 2009).
3. W. Raymond Wood, *Prologue to Lewis and Clark: The Mackay and Evans Expedition* (Norman: University of Oklahoma Press, 2003).
4. Ibid., xi.

James Webber, "Captn James Cook, F. R. S." in *A Voyage to the Pacific Ocean*, by James Cook and James King (London: G. Nicol and T. Cadell, 1784), frontispiece. This engraving of James Cook is from a drawing by Webber composed in 1776 at Cape Town early in Cook's third and final voyage. Courtesy of the Washington State Historical Society. WSHS 2011.0.60.3.5.1.

CHAPTER 1

LEWIS AND CLARK IN THE AGE OF COOK

James P. Ronda, in videotaped valedictory remarks at the 2013 Lewis and Clark Trail Heritage Foundation annual meeting in Bismarck, North Dakota, made two salient observations. The first was a restatement of a point he had made in many of his essays over the course of the previous two decades: that it was time—long past time—to put the Lewis and Clark Expedition in a comparative context. His second comment, emphasizing the more general point, was this: "It was not the age of Lewis and Clark," rather, "it was the age of Cook and Vancouver."[1] With this remark Ronda meant to reverse the polarity of common perception of the Lewis and Clark story which, when studied in juxtaposition to other expeditions, is neither as triumphal nor even the exceptional event it is often made out to be when studied in isolation. This axiom is even truer when we include Alexander Mackenzie in the equation.

James Cook made scientific exploration central to the intellectual life of the Enlightenment and inspired a generation. France's response took the form of Jean-François de Galaup, comte de La Pérouse's voyage, a largely vain attempt to expand on Cook's geographic discernment of the Pacific Basin. La Pérouse sailed from Brest in 1785, the year after Cook's third-voyage account of the search for the Northwest Passage was published to customary acclaim. His mission included looking for any interesting openings in the Northwest Coast that might become the long-sought passage. La Pérouse was skeptical about the prospects for finding any such thing (for the same reason Cook was, as explained below), though he did explore Lituya Bay in Alaska near 59°N. His principal contribution to geographic comprehension of the Pacific Basin came in his delineation of the coastline of East Asia, such as the Korean peninsula, the only part of the Pacific Basin Cook never explored (only because he was killed before he had a chance to do so).

Curiously, La Pérouse had an indirect influence on Spain's long-delayed response to Cook. When La Pérouse reached northern California in 1786, he broached to Spanish colonial officials there that he had just sailed into the increasingly contested waters of the North Pacific. Historically, the Spanish had been concerned about Russian fur trade incursions into their presumptive control of the basin at its northern perimeter, followed by the even more ominous appearance of Cook in that zone in 1778. Now even the French were engaged in the quest for the Northwest Passage. When Alejandro Malaspina's instructions were first drawn up over the winter of 1788–89, the Northwest Coast of America was not a part of his discovery agenda. Sailing from Cádiz in July 1789, Malaspina's two ships reached their staging station on the Pacific Coast of Mexico in late 1790 with the same general scientific agenda that had impelled the voyages of Cook and La Pérouse. But in Acapulco his instructions were amended with the directive to sail north, rather than toward the Philippines as had been intended. Not only had the French joined the British in a search for the Northwest Passage that was heating up again in what was formerly their backyard, the British were also now tussling with Spanish officials over trading prerogatives in Nootka Sound, first discovered by Cook and popularized as a sea otter haven in his third-voyage account.

So, in May 1791 Malaspina's two-ship flotilla dutifully sailed north. Feeling distracted, he did so more in resignation than with enthusiasm, and so too some of his men who nearly revolted at the prospect of sailing for Alaska instead of Hawaii. In any event, Malaspina reached as far north as Yakutat Bay. When he returned to Mexico at the end of that summer, he was eager to resume the original mission, only to find that the colonial officials there had learned of new inklings of the Strait of Juan de Fuca, recently "rediscovered" by Spanish navigators and British fur traders working out of Nootka Sound. Malaspina was ready to move on, thinking he had already squandered a season of exploration in higher latitudes, and in March 1792 he resumed his original course toward the Philippines. But before leaving Mexico he detached two of his best navigators, Dionisio Alcalá and Cayetano Valdés, who had sailed with him from Spain. In separate vessels they explored the strait and circumnavigated what was discerned and named Vancouver Island. Because the travels of Alcalá and Valdés had originated with Malaspina, their work in the inland waters of the Pacific Northwest is considered an adjunct of the latter's expedition.

Henry Roberts, *A General Chart Exhibiting the Discoveries made by Captn James Cook*, in *A Voyage to the Pacific Ocean*, by James Cook and James King (London: G. Nicol and T. Cadell, 1784), atlas, frontispiece. This map, prepared for inclusion in the official account of Cook's third voyage and published after his death, is the first modern map of the world. Initially intended to show the track of Cook's ships during all three voyages, the chart is noteworthy as a cartographic image because it was the earliest normative projection of the globe's surface in the sense that it provides a generally accurate depiction of the continental masses, especially in regard to the oceanic expanses that separate them. This was achieved by a rigorous adherence to gridlines depicting latitude and longitude, in contrast to its pre-Enlightenment predecessors, which were often decorated with fanciful representations of nautical mythologies and usually embellished by purely speculative geographies. Courtesy of the Washington State Historical Society. WSHS 2011.0.60.3.3.1.

In another curious twist, Alcalá and Valdés met George Vancouver in the summer of 1792 near the San Juan Islands. Vancouver had been sent to the Northwest Coast to negotiate an on-site settlement of contested claims with Spain at Nootka Sound, but having to go that far he was also given a discovery agenda. The numerous British fur traders who had followed Cook's track to the Northwest Coast were beginning to reveal a far more intricate coastline than Cook had reason to suspect, or need to discern. Extravagant claims, most famously those propagated by John Meares, about how far inland these various inlets extended, dictated a follow-up survey. In this fashion, Vancouver's expedition to the Northwest Coast (1792–94) preceded Lewis and Clark to the western end of their discovery zone, where their work overlapped Vancouver's. (See chapter 5.) Nonetheless, it was the Canadian fur trade explorer Alexander Mackenzie upon whom the American captains were the most reliant, as detailed in the next chapter.

But Cook was the progenitor of Northwest discovery and there we return. A few key themes will provide some flavor of what the Cook context of Lewis and Clark will yield by way of understanding and appreciation. Let's start with the historiography. Historians have been far too forgiving of Meriwether Lewis's idiosyncrasies and too critical of Cook's, at least in regard to his third and final voyage. Lewis consistently seized upon or manufactured the circumstances that allowed him to jump ahead of William Clark in pursuit of exploratory glory. He did this by proceeding in a solitary fashion to the junction of the Yellowstone and the Missouri; then later to the Pacific Ocean, while Clark was marooned with the detachment at Dismal Nitch; and most notoriously, by venturing on the quest for the Shoshones and the Continental Divide at Lemhi Pass. The Lemhi vanguard movement, which the journals of both captains unmistakably insinuate Clark intended to make, was compounded by Lewis's outright expropriation of geographic information from Clark's subsequent foray west of the divide. Lewis did this to make himself appear to be a more discerning explorer in narrative form than he was in practice. Even when Clark was the first to a noteworthy benchmark, such as the Three Forks of the Missouri, Lewis larded his account with such grandiose text about this long-wished-for spot and the naming of its constituent rivers after national leaders and their personal attributes that historians have invariably gravitated to Lewis's account of this accomplishment, not Clark's.

Cook, however, has been victimized by the scholarly community's fundamental misunderstanding of the third-voyage's mission, if not more

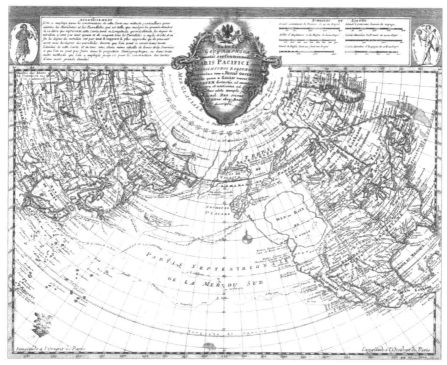

Leonhard Euler, *Tabula geographica partis Septenrionalis Maris Pacifici*, 1760. 15" h x 17" w.
This map, originally published in Berlin in 1753 and again in 1760 by Swiss mathematician Leonhard Euler (1707–83), appeared subsequent to, and is based upon, an image that
influential French cartographer Philippe Buache issued in 1752. Euler's *Atlas Geographicus
Omnes Orbis Terrarium Regiones in XLI Tabulis* contained forty-one double-paged maps, all
of which were based on the work of other cartographers, in this case Buache. In the wake
of Vitus Bering's recently completed voyages that drew the interest of geographers to the
North Pacific, both Buache and his occasional collaborator J. N. DeLisle issued dueling pro-
jections for the location of the Northwest Passage. Both versions included the long-standing
French cartographic notion of the *Mer de L'Ouest*, an imaginary analogue to Hudson Bay,
but Buache gave the concept its fullest expression. Conceived as a second-generation
Northwest Passage limiting the distance between the Atlantic and Pacific Basins, the *Mer
de L'Ouest* image outlasted James Cook, who thought his final voyage demolished the idea.
It was not fully vanquished until George Vancouver's three-year survey of the Northwest
Coast, 1792–94, during which he often mocked the idea of the "Mediterranean" of North
America. Courtesy of the Washington State Historical Society. WSHS 2003.16.19.

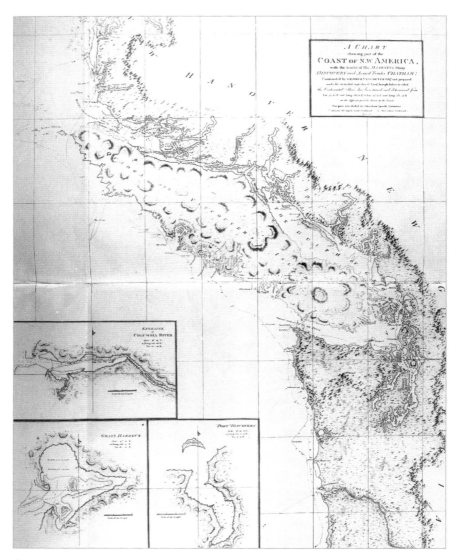

George Vancouver, *A Chart Showing part of the Coast of N. W. North America*. 1798. 22" h x 17" w. This chart displays the intricacy of Vancouver's survey of the Pacific Slope's mid-latitudes. This map was studied intently by Meriwether Lewis in preparation for his expedition and we know from his own account that he made a working copy of it. Courtesy of the Washington State Historical Society. WSHS 1911.5.4.

generally by the strictures of what I call the "Palm Tree Paradigm." This model reached its pure crystallized form in Tony Horwitz's *Blue Latitudes: Boldly Going Where Captain Cook Has Gone Before*.[2] Horwitz's topical and geographic orientation, as implied by the main title, suggests that the significance of Cook's exploratory ventures are to be understood within the context of the sandy beaches of Polynesia and the cross-cultural encounters that took place on those shores. This approach, informed by the European fascination with Polynesian exoticism that has dominated the study of Cook since the time of his voyages to the South Pacific, effectively wrote off Cook's more extensive reach (as measured by distance traveled or time sailed) into and along the icy, high latitudes of the Indian, Pacific, and Atlantic Oceans. Indeed, the actual missions of his second and third voyages were, respectively, the search for the rumored great southern continent (*Terra Australis Incognita*), followed by his quest for the equally elusive Northwest Passage in the North Pacific. During the course of his last two voyages, Cook occasionally called on the island paradises of the South Pacific, but they were merely his staging grounds, not the actual zone of discovery.

This has been compounded by the "Antipodal Axis" that dominates Cook studies, a paradigm that skews our understanding of Cook much in the same fashion that Lewis and Clark's Missouri River stories are privileged. This model of thought revolves around Great Britain, Cook's homeland and originating nation for the Greenwich meridian, and New Zealand and Australia, approximately on the opposite side of the globe. (Cook discovered and named the Antipodes, an island chain southeast of New Zealand precisely opposite Greenwich, England.) During his first voyage, which was initiated in the multinational effort to track the transit of Venus in 1769, Cook delineated New Zealand's insularity and the east coast of Australia. Given his centrality to those dominions becoming a part of the British Empire, much of the Cook documentary record came to be found in the cultural repositories of those countries. More importantly and characteristically, John C. Beaglehole, the editor of Cook's journals and the author of the most oft-cited biography of the man, was a New Zealander. The Northwest Passage, by definition a North American geographic perplex, is a distant and alien place from the British and Southwest Pacific centers of Cook studies, explaining why it is frequently dispatched with brevity in books that purport to be a comprehensive analysis of the great navigator's work.

Worse, in his annotation of the journals and in his biography of Cook, Beaglehole laid down the outlines of what has become a rigid interpretive orthodoxy about Cook generally and the third voyage in particular. Bea-glehole considered Cook's undertaking of the third voyage a mistake, if not a disaster. The specific shape of his critique takes the form of the three Fs: fatigue, friction, and failure, a typology that is mine but a lens through which we can see the effect of Beaglehole. Let's take these themes in turn.

Beaglehole was the first to hint that Cook was worn out by his first two voyages to the South Pacific. That led him to suggest that Cook never should have allowed himself to be talked into taking command of what would prove to be his last voyage so soon upon returning from the second in 1775. Bea-glehole perceived inklings of fatigue in Cook during his last swing through the South Pacific when, having gleaned knowledge of the islands of Samoa and Fiji, he deigned not to explore them further. Beaglehole, who hailed from New Zealand, seems to have taken this as an affront to the Southwest Pacific, asserting that the Cook of old, that is, the one from the first two voy-ages, would not have missed an opportunity to follow up on leads like this.

What Beaglehole, and most historians who have followed him, have failed to appreciate, is how devoted Cook was to the notion of fidelity to mission. Because of the time required to travel the great distance to the Northwest Coast of America from Great Britain (which involved following the generally westerly winds across the Indian Ocean to New Zealand and Tahiti in the South Pacific), Cook's third-voyage instructions specifically advised him to avoid distractions along the way, in Polyne-sia or elsewhere. Cook needed little convincing along these lines, having declared in his second-voyage journal near the end of the three-year cir-cumnavigation of Antarctica that he was "done" with the South Pacific.[3] In a sense, Cook had become bored by the prosaic work of outlining a seemingly limitless number of insular groups in the vast Pacific. He began gravitating instead toward what might be called a continental framework, in the form of a passage through or above and around North America, a goal of Columbian proportions.

Taking their cue from Beaglehole's diminished explorer hypothesis, historians of the Pacific Northwest have casually applied his argument to Cook's explorations of the Pacific Slope of America. It has long been an orthodox understanding of regional history that when Cook glided past the outfalls of what would later be denominated as the Columbia River and the Strait of Juan de Fuca, he supposedly missed these mid-latitude open-ings into the continent. In truth, the British Admiralty specifically advised

Cook not to begin to look for a Northwest Passage until he reached 65°N. This was sensible guidance. In the early 1770s, Hudson's Bay Company fur trade explorer Samuel Hearne reached the mouth of the Coppermine River where it emptied into the Arctic Ocean at what was calculated to be 72°N. Hearne had actually only made it to 68°N, but the larger point was that on his outbound route and subsequent return to Hudson Bay via the eastern extent of Great Slave Lake he had literally walked over any conceivable temperate-latitude corridor that might hold a passage from the Pacific to the Atlantic. Bearing this knowledge, and wary of losing time in what was to him a backwater region, Cook stopped along the Northwest Coast only to restore his ships and replenish his supplies at Nootka Sound. This inlet was later discerned to be part of an island named after its principal delineator, George Vancouver. (La Pérouse directly secured Hearne's insight about the impossibility of a mid-latitude saltwater passage from the Pacific to the Atlantic when he conquered Hearne's fort on Hudson Bay in 1781.)

A concomitant aspect of Cook's supposed fatigue during his third voyage was his increasingly fractious relationship with fellow crew members and South Pacific islanders. Regarding the latter, it may be fairly said that the rigors of managing the cultural encounter in Polynesia took its toll on Cook during the third voyage, but there is nothing in the documentary record relative to his dealings with Native people in the Northwest, Alaska, and Siberia to conclude that there was an endemic lack of cross-cultural sensitivity on his part. As for his shipboard colleagues, the conceit of Cook scholarship, as first put forth by Beaglehole but replicated endlessly since, is that the only variable on the final voyage is Cook himself. A fair reading and comparison of the journals for all three voyages indicates that Cook was dealing with a younger, less experienced, and more irritable set of officers and seamen during his final expedition. For instance, there were increased attempts at desertion (anticipating the mutiny on the *Bounty* in the ensuing decade), plus a large number of illicit journals that crept into print in the wake of the last voyage, despite specific directives from the British Admiralty proscribing it. Also, it is worth noting that Cook left England for the last time in July 1776, when the rebellion in the colonies was both draining the pool of available talent and exemplifying the spirit of an anti-authoritarian era that would reach a crescendo with the French Revolution in 1789.

In the same way that the early post-expeditionary death of Meriwether Lewis clouds the historiography of his venture with Clark, any expedition that ends with its commander dead is, by definition, less than fully successful. Still, Cook's third-voyage discoveries in the North Pacific, once he vacated what to him became the worked-over precincts of the South Pacific (Beaglehole's modern protest notwithstanding), were extraordinary by any measure, and deemed by his contemporaries as the most noteworthy of his career. A short list includes the detection and charting of the Hawaiian Islands, the trend line of the northwestern quadrant of the North American coastline, and the shape of the Alaskan subcontinent, including the specific delineation of the distance separating Siberia from North America at the Bering Strait. The strategic value of the Hawaiian archipelago, from its first sighting by Cook in January 1778 to this very day, is self-evident. His general depiction of the Pacific coast north of California and the Alaskan subcontinent to above the Arctic Circle stands as a distinct accomplishment in contrast to the fanciful notions that predominated in geographic circles in the centuries, indeed, in the few decades prior to his last expedition. As late as the 1740s, British armchair geographer Arthur Dobbs imagined a Pacific coastline that ran in a northeasterly direction from Cape Arago on the southern Oregon coast toward Baffin Bay west of Greenland.

Perhaps least appreciated of Cook's major findings, drawing on the proximity of the continents at the Bering Strait and the commonalities between Native people on either side of this watery divide, is that his third voyage popularized what has come down through time as the Bering land-bridge theory for the populating of the Western Hemisphere. These were not small accomplishments or ideas. And, as for not finding the Northwest Passage because he met with impenetrable ice: can the inability to find what does not (or at least prior to global warming, did not) exist be deemed a failure? Disproving the existence of the great southern continent made Cook the toast of Europe and not finding a shortcut to Europe should not have diminished the man's reputation. Had Cook not been killed overwintering in Hawaii after what he envisioned as his *first* season of Arctic exploration, it is doubtful that the failed third-voyage trope would have ever taken root. Besides which, Cook was never more vigorous nor perhaps as daring an explorer as when he coasted along the Arctic ice pack and probed the depths of Alaska's Norton Sound looking for a way around the ice and across the top of North America.

My point, returning to Ronda: there is every bit as much of a need for a new look at Cook as there is for fresh perspectives upon the Lewis and

Clark story, and separately I have responded to that challenge.[4] Ronda once perceptively averred that at its root exploration history is really environmental history.[5] This assertion is particularly relevant to Cook because if he was voyaging north through the Bering Strait and the archipelago of northern Canada in 2020 instead of 1778, he would have found his way through to Baffin Bay and out Davis Strait near Greenland and back to England. Global warming, without prejudice to the debate over the origins of the same, is ineluctably creating the very same passage that eluded Cook. The great navigator's high-latitude exploits amid snow and ice are, for our time, far more relevant than sandy beach crossings and the anthropological debates that surround them.

In this way, seeing Lewis and Clark as part of the "Age of Cook" also puts the American overland expedition into the widest possible context: Enlightenment-era exploration and, more specifically, the search for the Northwest Passage, one of the two great concerns of that age, the other being *Terra Australis Incognita*. It is frequently stated that the Lewis and Clark Expedition proved the nonexistence of the passage, but this is a simplistic understanding. The concept of the Northwest Passage evolved over time and it actually continues to evolve.

Captain Cook proved for his time that a high-latitude saltwater passage from the North Pacific to the North Atlantic did not exist. Cook was followed by Vancouver, who had sailed on Cook's last two voyages. Much like Cook's third-voyage record has been accreted with myth, so too has Vancouver's expedition. The common misunderstanding is that Vancouver was sent to finish the survey and make up for the deficiencies that Cook, a supposedly fatigued and lessened explorer, left uninvestigated. In fact, Vancouver was sent on a completely different mission: to find a temperate-latitude Pacific analogue to Hudson Bay, an old cartographic concept that was first made popular in French geographic circles and called the *Mer de L'Ouest*. The thinking behind Vancouver's voyage was that this North American "Mediterranean," accessed off the Pacific, would facilitate a communication with the lakes of Canada or Hudson Bay, creating a de facto passage that British fur-trading interests could dominate. Vancouver's explorations from 1792–94 demolished that idea.

No *idée fixe* in North American history has been more durable than the Northwest Passage and thus its image evolved to a concourse of rivers. This vision was first articulated by the American-born but Canadian-employed fur trade explorer Peter Pond. Inspired by Cook's geographic discernments and perhaps more particularly by the promise of marketing North American furs in the Chinese market (a prospect Cook's crew stumbled upon near the end of the third voyage), Pond gradually expanded his range of operations in the 1780s to the Canadian Northwest first touched by Hearne a decade earlier. Pond's problematic relations with business partners truncated his efforts in the fur-rich Athabasca District, but he was able to pass his transcontinental vision to a fellow trader, Alexander Mackenzie. This phase of the Northwest Passage is, of course, the one of which Lewis and Clark are a part, having been dispatched by Thomas Jefferson in response to the Mackenzie expedition that reached Pacific tidewater in 1793. Like Cook, Vancouver, and Mackenzie, Lewis and Clark also failed to find a practicable version of the passage, their best efforts notwithstanding. It was not until the fourth version, the one instituted severally by the Northern Pacific, Canadian Pacific, and Great Northern railroads, that the functional equivalent of a passage was finally realized. Of course, as intimated above, in our time a new, and now fifth, Northwest Passage is becoming real, one which, in a few centuries, if the pace of warming continues, will truly serve as the "Northern Mediterranean."

Let me conclude by offering one last reflection on Cook and Lewis and Clark's mentor, Thomas Jefferson. In one of the great coincidences in history, Cook was preparing to leave Portsmouth, England, for what would prove to be the last time, the same month that Jefferson inscribed the Declaration of Independence. Indeed, Cook saw the ships in the neighboring slips filling up with arms and men intended for the Atlantic side of America at precisely the same time he was preparing to venture to the far Pacific coast of the same continent. Historians, generally, have done a bad job of introducing "contingency" to their narratives and the attendant perspective such sensibility can bring. So, let us hark back to Beaglehole and his implied premise that Cook should have stayed home and enjoyed his retirement and not undertaken his third and final voyage. Is it conceivable that one of Britain's greatest naval masters and commanders would have sat out the war with the colonies? The implication of Barbara Tuchman's *The First Salute*[6] is that, from the time of John Paul Jones's (of "we have not yet begun to fight" fame) significant battle off Cook's native Yorkshire coast early in the war to the British naval debacle in the run-up to Yorktown that brought it to an end, the British needed only one capable, energetic naval leader to counter the American rebels and the French navy. The rebellion might have been put down or concluded in a fashion distinct from outright American independence, but the Royal Navy's best captain (who was on a career track that would have made him an admiral) was instead in the North Pacific. Either way, it seems, James Cook was destined to make history in the last half of the 1770s. It was, truly, the Age of Cook.

———— NOTES ————

1. This essay is based on a presentation at the Forty-Fifth Meeting of the Lewis and Clark Trail Heritage Foundation, Bismarck, North Dakota, July 31, 2013, at which Ronda's remarks were presented via videotape.
2. Tony Horwitz, *Blue Latitudes: Boldly Going Where Captain Cook Has Gone Before* (New York: Picador/Henry Holt, 2002).
3. John C. Beaglehole, ed., *The Journals of Captain James Cook on His Voyages of Discovery* (Cambridge: Cambridge University Press, 1961), 2: 587.
4. David L. Nicandri, *Captain Cook Rediscovered: Voyaging in the Icy Latitudes* (Vancouver: University of British Columbia Press, 2020).
5. James P. Ronda, "Counting Cats in Zanzibar, or, Lewis and Clark Reconsidered," *Western Historical Quarterly*, 33: 1 (Spring 2002): 15.
6. Barbara Tuchman, *The First Salute: A View of the American Revolution* (New York: Knopf, 1988).

Thomas Lawrence, *Alexander Mackenzie, Esqr,* in *Voyages from Montreal*, by Alexander Mackenzie (London: T. Cadell, 1801), frontispiece. Courtesy of the Washington State Historical Society. WSHS 1975.131.1.1.

CHAPTER 2

EXPLORING UNDER THE INFLUENCE OF ALEXANDER MACKENZIE

The bicentennial commemoration of Meriwether Lewis and William Clark's voyage precipitated such an enormous amount of literature that even before its conclusion a historian suggested that the captains' journals had been completely mined of scholarly meaning. However, this claim proved premature. The truth of the matter is that the publication of the modern, comprehensive edition of their journals published by Gary E. Moulton between 1983 and 2001 is still a relatively recent historiographic development. Indeed, the journals' documentary record as interpretable text is only beginning to be read. As an analogue, consider that John C. Beaglehole published the journals of Captain Cook between 1955 and 1967 and the contents of those volumes still attract vibrant study.

Furthermore, the hagiographic tendency within the literature discussing Lewis and Clark has occluded a principal point: the American captains did not operate in a vacuum. Drawing on the foundation provided by James P. Ronda's *Lewis and Clark among the Indians* (1984), one salutary aspect of the bicentennial studies was their inclusion of the tribal side of the story. Nonetheless, the expedition launched by Thomas Jefferson also took place within imperial and literary contexts that are often overlooked. Alexander Mackenzie's explorations in 1789 and 1793, in furtherance of British commercial interests as a partner in the North West Company operating out of Montreal, and his narrative published in 1801, figure prominently in regard to both of these circumstances. Mackenzie's biographer characterized his voyages as "two gigantic thrusts into the unknown." In so doing, Mackenzie served as "the pioneer of transcontinental exploration north of the Rio Grande," but his account, on close inspection, was also a methodological and literary model for Lewis and Clark.[1]

Having replicated Alexander Mackenzie's transcontinental feat by reaching the mouth of the Columbia River, William Clark asked his mates on the evening of November 17, 1805, if there was anyone "who wished to See more of the main *Ocian*." This phrasing is telling because it suggests the party considered Station Camp, the westernmost site the party reached as a whole, to be on the Pacific; this despite the fact that it was nearly ten miles inland from the ocean (near present-day Chinook, Washington). Today's visual experience inside the bar of the Columbia River is deceiving because a jetty juts into the ocean nearly six miles from Oregon's Point Adams, creating a sense of enclosure that would not have been apparent two centuries ago. Clark's query, combined with all the maritime-oriented words in the journals and the outright expression of having a full, plain view of the sea, indicates that he and the balance of the company were under the distinct impression that the oceanic goal of the expedition had been reached and that they were not situated merely on the lower stretch of the Columbia River. Indeed, in response to his query, Clark reported that two-thirds of the crew were "contented with what part of the Ocean & its curiosities which Could be Seen from the vicinity of our Camp."[2]

Ten men accompanied Clark on this sojourn to the "main Ocian" commencing the next day, including Sergeants John Ordway and Nathaniel Pryor, the Field brothers (Joseph and Reubin), George Shannon, the ineffable John Colter, Toussaint Charbonneau, and York, the West's first African American explorer and Clark's slave. Proceeding west along the north bank of the Columbia, Clark was careful to sustain his map work by continuing his course and distance calculations, including a backsight of "Camp Point," known today as Chinook Point within present-day Fort Columbia State Park. The area between "a bluff of yellow Clay" (still visible from the Port of Ilwaco) and the foot of Cape Disappointment was the area "in which the nativs inform us the Ships anchor, and from whence they receive their goods in return for their peltries." Several of Clark's maps of the vicinity depict symbols of anchors or ships in the deep arm of Baker Bay.[3]

At this harbor Clark "found Capt Lewis name on a tree," Lewis having preceded him to this spot by four days. Following Lewis's lead, Clark engraved his "name & by land the day of the month and year, as also Several of the men." Lewis had probably chosen this tree because of its proximity to the preferred anchorage of the intermittent coastal traders. Inscribing his name would prove the success of his and Clark's voyage across the continent to any subsequent passerby. We do not know the exact scripting of Lewis's carving but as explained below Clark consciously modeled his text after the notation Mackenzie left on a rock at Bella Coola on the British Columbia coast in 1793.[4]

The figure of Alexander Mackenzie, a native of Scotland and a fur trader for the Canadian-based North West Company, is regularly invoked relative to the origins of the American Expedition for Northwestern Discovery. Less appreciated is how his geographical memoir, *Voyages from Montreal*, affected the narrative manner and content of the Lewis and Clark journals once the captains were in the field. As detailed in this essay, in some respects it appears that *Voyages* served as a stylistic and tactical guide for Lewis and Clark. Besides making inscriptions on trees, the Americans used a number of Mackenzie's field maneuvers, as may have been expected, but perhaps more substantively they emulated, and even plagiarized, many textual passages.[5]

Alexander Mackenzie's report of his successive voyages to the Arctic in 1789 and the Pacific in 1793 first appeared in print in London in October 1801. Jefferson read Mackenzie's narrative in 1802. By all accounts, the president was prompted into the venture that became the Lewis and Clark Expedition by Mackenzie's strategic flourish in the volume's concluding paragraphs. Conjoining his own transcontinental survey with George Vancouver's coastal reconnaissance (1792–94), Mackenzie described an imperial vision positing the Columbia River as the key "line of communication… pointed out by nature" across the continent between the Atlantic and the Pacific. Furthermore, "its banks also form…the most Northern situation fit for colonization, and suitable to the residence of a civilized people. By opening the intercourse between the Atlantic and Pacific Oceans, and forming regular establishments through the interior, and at both extremes…the entire command of the fur trade of North America might be obtained."[6]

The "intercourse between the Atlantic and Pacific Oceans" was a coded reference to the Northwest Passage, a centuries-old geographic image dating to William Baffin and Henry Hudson in the early seventeenth century and explored more recently by James Cook in 1778 and George Vancouver. All of these explorers failed to find the passage, but the concept was an enduring idea and Mackenzie transformed the model from navigable seas (which Cook sought) and saltwater shortcuts (Vancouver's mission) to a network of rivers. To Jefferson, Mackenzie's vision was a grave threat to

American commercial aspirations because he painted his imperial picture in starkly competitive terms. The fur trade, Mackenzie said, was a "field for commercial enterprise, and incalculable would be the produce of it, when supported by the operations of that credit and capital which Great Britain so pre-eminently possesses." This strategic plan would preempt the "American adventurers," Mackenzie sneered, "who without regularity or capital, or the desire of conciliatory future confidence, look altogether to the interest of the moment."[7]

Mackenzie's *Voyages* was so important that Lewis and Clark carried a copy with them. We know this because scholars have detected references to tribes in Lewis and Clark's documentary record that were encountered by Mackenzie (but not by the captains) plus technical information about the fur trade that they also secured from the Scotsman. In a report sent downstream from the 1804–5 overwintering site among the Mandan and Hidatsa Indians and subsequently published in New Orleans in July 1805, Lewis credited Mackenzie with accurately charting the area around Fort Mandan. However, Mackenzie had not mapped that particular area; Lewis was probably referring to a section in Mackenzie's journal in which he reported on the upper Missouri River explorations of David Thompson.[8]

More subtly and without acknowledgment, Mackenzie's narrative clearly informed several intriguing passages in the journals of Lewis and Clark. Consider for example Clark's mysterious reference to Captain Cook's assertion that canoes on the Northwest Coast had human teeth embedded in their surface for ornamental purposes. Clark, in his journal entry for the first full day of travel after leaving Fort Clatsop in the spring of 1806, criticized Cook for not paying closer attention to ethnographic detail because two canoes Clark saw were festooned with shells, not teeth, as he supposed Cook had asserted. This literary affair will be more fully explicated in a later chapter, but suffice to say here that it was not Cook who was the source of Clark's observation, but Mackenzie. In short, Clark appropriated Mackenzie's (ultimately misguided) decorative insight without attribution, correcting the great Cook by name. Clark seems to have kept Mackenzie's role hidden for strategic reasons.[9]

There are many other instances suggesting Lewis and Clark emulated Mackenzie's conduct besides the most obvious case of inscribing their names to mark the end of the voyage. On the more prosaic side of things, we find for example that Lewis added a dog to his entourage. Like Lewis's Seaman, Mackenzie's mascot (also a Newfoundland dog) appears in the narrative, alternately hunting, patrolling the perimeter of campsites, acting playful, and getting lost.[10]

If, as has been argued, Lewis and Clark changed their clothing on November 8, 1805, in anticipation of a ceremonial arrival at what they thought might prove the end of their outbound voyage, including a possible encounter with the captain of a fur-trading vessel, they may have been inspired by Mackenzie's tactics. In his narrative, Mackenzie described preparations for a "becoming appearance" at a post. Choreographing an impressive advent was very much a tradition in the fur trade of which Mackenzie was a part. Shortly before his arrival at Pacific tidewater, Mackenzie shaved and changed his "linen," urging his mates to follow this "humanising example." A recent account has suggested that Lewis and Clark had similar intentions, although in the first published edition of the journals, as paraphrased by Nicholas Biddle, Clark asserted that the change of clothes at Pillar Rock was the function of a more quotidian concern: their garments were simply wet.[11]

The first time Mackenzie employed the imperial rite of inscription that Lewis and Clark later found so compelling was in 1789 at the mouth of the river that now bears his name where it meets the Arctic Ocean. There he engraved his name, size of party, and date of arrival. When Mackenzie reached his western terminus four years later, he described with greater flourish yet another moment of exploratory triumph. "I now mixed up some vermilion in melted grease, and inscribed, in large characters, on the South-East face of the rock on which we had slept last night, this brief memorial—'Alexander Mackenzie, from Canada, by land, the twenty-second of July, one thousand seven hundred and ninety-three.'" Allowing for the change in persona and date, this is the textual formula Clark followed. Interestingly, Mackenzie's westernmost point of observation on a rocky outcrop in the Dean Channel, an arm of the ocean, had a far more constricted view of the Pacific, if even that, than the American expedition had at Station Camp.[12]

Whereas Lewis appears to have marked his name on trees only twice, Clark did so more than a dozen times and on one occasion he used the same type of red paint as Mackenzie had at Bella Coola on the British Columbia coast. If there is a pattern to Clark's behavior, it seems he was compelled to inscribe his name when Lewis had jumped ahead of the main party in pursuit of exploratory claims (thus signifying that he was present too) or in the few instances when he was in the lead himself. Accordingly, the Clark inscriptions are bunched together. He left two at the approach to, and the traverse of, the Great Falls of the Missouri, one along the Salmon River in Idaho, and four on the Pacific Coast. On the return voyage, he left four along the Yellowstone River, one of which is his famed engraving on Pompeys Pillar.[13]

Stephen E. Ambrose fashioned the apparently fictive notion that Lewis took Mackenzie's name on a rock as "a direct, open, irresistible challenge." There is no explicit documentary evidence to support this assertion, but as speculation the premise might better be applied to Clark who, as a former frontier surveyor, would have been more naturally accustomed to the practice of marking claims and survey corners. Although historians have always been more intrigued by Lewis's idiosyncrasies, this one of Clark's merits further attention. Clark may have figured that Lewis was destined to leave his mark with the published account of the expedition and thus this rustic practice was a compensating recourse. Thomas P. Slaughter theorized that Lewis and Clark inscribed their names to reassure themselves in the face of the supposedly "devastating news" that other English-speaking explorers had reached the mouth of the Columbia River before they did. According to Slaughter, Lewis and Clark tried to hide this fact from prospective readers of their account.[14]

What Slaughter suggests would have been impossible to do in practice and is a silly proposition besides. More credibly, John Logan Allen observes that the expedition's acquisition of Mackenzie's *Voyages* for the expedition's library was much more meaningful to Clark than Lewis. The reason, Allen argued, is that the latter had been a student of continental geography long before the expedition, while to Clark, who had spent more of his life on the western frontier, much in Mackenzie's account would have been revelatory. Within that context William H. Goetzmann wrote: "Despite Clark's scientific dedication, imperial rivalries were not far from his mind."[15]

Thus, the intentional phrasing of Clark's rejoinder that he wrote on a tree at the Pacific coast seems almost purposively transparent. Such cannot be said for Meriwether Lewis's use of Mackenzie. Stephen Dow Beckham noted that a "faint echo" of Mackenzie can be found in Lewis's miscellaneous reports dispatched from Fort Mandan. In truth, Lewis borrowed heavily from Mackenzie at regular intervals, never with attribution, in both the structure of his own narrative and writing style. Although the scientific ethos of the Enlightenment was still the dominant cultural fashion of the late eighteenth century of Cook, Vancouver, Mackenzie, and Jefferson, there were other intellectual currents still at play. Lewis came to maturity

in an era that Percy G. Adams once characterized as "an age of plagiarism."
This tradition, now nearly completely lost sight of by scholars, frustrated
the empirical quest for accuracy and objectivity. It took root "when voyagers, imbued with a real or supposed desire to be thorough...read other
travelers or geographers and then shamelessly plagiarized them."[16]

Though Lewis never had the chance to acknowledge this and other
problematic aspects of exploration literature because of his early death,
Mackenzie, to his credit, did. He warned his readers "not to expect the
charms of embellished narrative, or animated description." Nevertheless,
Mackenzie, like John Meares before him, was assisted in the preparation
of his account by one William Combe. W. Kaye Lamb, after comparing
Combe's enhancements to Mackenzie's original wording, determined that
the basic chronology and sequence of events went undisturbed, but many
grammatical changes were made and "purple patches" added. It turns out
Lewis had a secret ghostwriter too—Mackenzie himself.[17]

Lewis is now well known for his spotty journal keeping and, subsequent
to the completion of the voyage, writer's block. That someone who clearly
struggled with his writing secretly sought the aid of another author should
therefore hardly seem surprising. As Derek Hayes noted, in the era of Mackenzie and Lewis "a somewhat more flowery language was in vogue." If a
compelling narrative and literary embellishment was part of what an explorer
delivered to his waiting audience, then what, really, was Lewis to do?[18]

As noted above, Jefferson read *Voyages* with great interest but surely he
did not study it more avidly than Lewis did. Thomas P. Slaughter argues
that Lewis created a fictional identity "based on the idealizations of other
explorers." According to Slaughter, many explorers' stylized narratives say
more about "the standards against which they measured themselves than
about who they are." Lewis's more reflective and elaborately composed
notebook journal entries, which give every appearance of being the first
draft of the expected published account and not a mere field log, substantiate Slaughter's theory.[19]

Consider first one of the most romantic passages in Lewis's oeuvre, the
oft-quoted paragraphs written, as is commonly supposed, at the time of
the expedition's departure from Fort Mandan in April 1805. Comparing
his venture with those of Columbus and Cook, Lewis admitted to giving
vent to his imagination, which wandered "into futurity." The picture in his
mind "was a most pleasing one. [E]ntertaining as I do, the most confident
hope of succeeding in a voyage which had formed a *da[r]ling project* of

mine for the last ten years, I could but esteem this moment of my departure as among the most happy of my life"[20] (emphasis added).

Having the luxury of an entire winter to prepare for the moment when
he would inscribe this entry, Lewis carefully contemplated how to compose
it. After all, he had not written a continuous journal since the previous September. With Mackenzie's *Voyages* at hand, he would have read the Scot's
thoughtful reflection at an equally propitious moment in June 1793—the
abandonment of what the fur trader thought was the Great River of the
West (named Columbia a year earlier by Robert Gray, but actually the
Fraser River) for an alternate overland route to the Pacific Ocean. On that
occasion, Mackenzie wrote of "contriving means to bring about a recon-
ciliation with the natives, which alone would enable me to procure guides,
without whose assistance it would be impossible for me to proceed, when
my *darling project* would end in disappointment"[21] (emphasis added).

While at Fort Mandan Lewis seems to have emulated Mackenzie on
a more vital matter. Before referring to Columbus and Cook, Lewis wrote
about securing the services of a tribal ambassador. Entering an extent of
country west of Fort Mandan that had seen few if any white men, Lewis
and Clark signed on a man of the Mandan nation to accompany them "as
far as the Snake Indians with a view to bring about a good understanding
and friendly intercourse." This fellow, it turns out, abandoned Lewis and
Clark two days later. In this respect, the captains were extraordinarily fortunate, because no tribal encounters took place until they were nigh upon the
Continental Divide. However, from that crest to The Dalles on the Columbia the expedition was guided by a succession of pilots, namely Old Toby
of the Shoshone and the Nez Perce chiefs Twisted Hair and Tetoharsky.[22]

Mackenzie wrote extensively about the value of having a "conductor" in the party, by which he meant a local Native who could be cajoled,
bribed, or forced to accompany the expedition. In his strongest statement
in this vein, Mackenzie said that "attempting the woods, without a guide,
to introduce us to the first inhabitants, such a determination would be
little short of absolute madness." The strategy paid dividends frequently. In
one instance, Mackenzie persuaded two tribesmen to accompany him to
"secure…a favourable reception from their neighbours." On another occasion, word of Mackenzie's approach had preceded him, so the "conductors"
went ahead to the next village "on an embassy of friendship." During the
final push to the coast at Bella Coola, the Indians with the party proposed,
Mackenzie wrote, "to send two young men on before us, to notify to the

different tribes that we were approaching, that they might not be surprised at our appearance, and be disposed to afford us a friendly reception."[23]

Similarly, the not-so-faint echo of Mackenzie's voice can be detected in the succession of key events on the voyage west from Fort Mandan—the decision at the Marias River, the portage of the Great Falls, the crossing of the divide, the startling incidents with tribes on the Columbia who had never seen white men, the arrival at the Pacific, plus the march through the Bitterroots on the return trip. At the first of these places, Lewis and Clark insisted, against the opinion of every other member of the party, that the western, or what the captains referred to as the "South," fork of the Missouri was the main stem of the river. To address this geographic crisis, Clark and Lewis made a separate reconnaissance—Clark of the Missouri and Lewis of the Marias—to assess the situation. In the end, the men swallowed their reservations and fell into line behind the captains. In his memorable description of this moment, Lewis wrote that the men "said very cheerfully that they were ready to follow us any wher[e] we thought proper to direct but that they still thought that the other was the river."[24]

In three instances, Mackenzie had used nearly identical tactics and language to describe the same group dynamic. In the Arctic in the summer of 1789, when doubt crept into the minds of the party members about whether they would reach the sea, circumstances dictated that Mackenzie try to boost morale. Surely, he suggested to his men, the expedition would soon reach the ocean. In response, Mackenzie wrote, they "declare themselves now and at any time ready to go with me wherever I choose to lead them."[25]

There were two decisions like the one the captains made at the Marias during Mackenzie's trek to the Pacific Ocean in 1793. Approaching the divide by way of the Peace River, Mackenzie's party came to a large fork created by tributary streams now named the Parsnip and Finlay Rivers, presenting themselves from the north and south. Mackenzie ordered his steersman up the southern, or Parsnip, branch. Immediately, everyone in the party, fur traders and Indian guides alike, objected to Mackenzie's decision. After a difficult two or three miles—what Mackenzie called "a very tardy and mortifying progress"—the party came to a halt. He determined that the hard work and risk inherent in his decision to take the fork with the more rapid flow "required some degree of consideration." Which is to say, Mackenzie consulted the party. Explaining his reasoning, Mackenzie said he employed "those arguments which were the best calculated to calm their immediate discontents, as well as to encourage their future hopes." Similarly,

Lewis's arguments in favor of his preferred fork of the Missouri "endeavoured to impress on the minds of the party" that the commander was correct. He cited directional bearings, his analysis of mountain and plains topography, and information he had gleaned from Indians near Fort Mandan about the navigability and clarity of the water forming the Missouri's true source. In so doing, Lewis employed a Mackenzian style of field instruction.[26]

After Mackenzie crossed the divide, discretion required him to abandon the idea of a southerly voyage down the Fraser River because of a canyon later called Hell Gate. To avoid that narrow snare, Mackenzie settled on an overland trail to the west. Once again, after an appeal to "their fortitude, patience, and perseverance," Mackenzie's men "unanimously assured me, that they were as willing now as they had ever been, to abide by my resolutions, whatever they might be, and to follow me wherever I should go."[27]

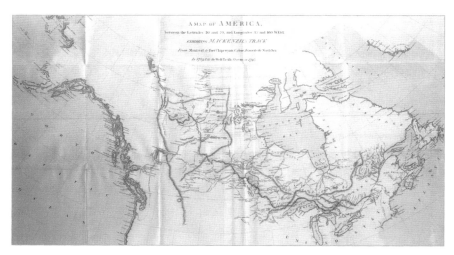

A Map of America between the Latitudes 40 and 70, and Longitudes 45 and 180 West: Exhibiting Mackenzie's Track from Montreal to Fort Chipewyan, & from thence to the North Sea in 1789, & to the West Pacific Ocean [sic] in 1793, in *Voyages from Montreal*, by Alexander Mackenzie (London: T. Cadell, 1801). 23" h x 32" w. A revised version of this map in 1802, prepared by famed British cartographer Aaron Arrowsmith (and corrected to note Mackenzie's track to the North Pacific), was in Lewis and Clark's travelling library. This chart reflected the geographic insights gleaned from both Mackenzie on his voyages to the Arctic in 1789 and Pacific in 1793 and George Vancouver's survey of the Northwest Coast, and was the sum total of geographic comprehension of the northwest quadrant of the continent prior to the Lewis and Clark Expedition. Courtesy of the Washington State Historical Society. WSHS 1918.115.8.1.

Arguably, the most famous and florid passages in the entirety of Lewis's oeuvre is his nearly poetic description of the Great Falls of the Missouri. Attempting to paint a picture with words, Lewis wrote some of his most memorable lines. A few shall suffice. The first set of falls Lewis happened upon were, he said, "the grandest sight I ever beheld...the water in it's passage down...assumes a thousand forms in a moment sometimes flying up in jets of sparkling foam." Adjoining the falls there was "a handsom little bottom of about three acres which is deversified and agreeably shaded with some cottonwood trees," plus "a few small cedar grow near the ledge of rocks where I rest." Lewis marveled at "the reflection of the sun on the spray or mist which arrises from these falls" and the "beatiful rainbow produced which adds not a little to the beauty of this majestically grand senery."[28]

The next day, as Lewis continued his tour of the falls, he came to another cascade, which he billed "one of the most beatifull objects in nature." Comparing the two, Lewis concluded that this second of "two great rivals for glory...was *pleasingly beautifull,* while the other was *sublimely grand.*"[29]

Working in the idiom of the travel narrative, Lewis was expected to encounter and describe wonders of nature. Not knowing whether he would see even more spectacular sights, he strained to apply every colorful phrase his mind could compose. For inspiration, he drew on the literature of Captain Cook (described in a separate chapter) and Mackenzie. The latter had described his encounters with the sublime in the history of the fur trade to introduce the account of his trips to the Arctic and Pacific Oceans. *Voyages* contained a comparably exotic scene: the Methye Portage near the present northern border between Alberta and Saskatchewan. The final precipice of the portage, Mackenzie wrote, rising "upwards of a thousand feet above the plain beneath it, commands a most extensive, romantic and ravishing prospect." This valley, he continued, "at once refreshed and adorned by [the Clearwater River], is about three miles in breadth,...displaying a most delightful intermixture of wood and lawn, and stretching on till the blue mist obscures the prospect." Like Lewis's favorite "neighbourhood," Mackenzie's was a park for game, "where the elk and buffalo find pasture." "Nor," Mackenzie concluded, "when I beheld this wonderful display of uncultivated nature, was the moving scenery of human occupation wanting to complete the picture."[30]

In his famous coda to the romantic grandeur that he found at the falls, Lewis wrote that on reviewing his text he became so "disgusted with the imperfect idea which it conveyed of the scene that I determined to draw my pen across it and begin agin." Lewis wished that he "might be enabled to give to the enlightened world some just idea of this truly magnificent and sublimely grand object." Before fixing his camp for the day, Lewis quickly sketched the scene to later aid his recollection of a landscape that filled him "at this moment…with such pleasure and astonishment."[31]

Lewis's purported literary limitations, known to students of travel literature as the trope of ineffability, inscribed a sense of literary drama, which also echoes Mackenzie's style in *Voyages*. Shortly after starting his ascent of the Peace River in the spring of 1793, Mackenzie had his epiphany in nature, a few days east of the present British Columbia–Alberta border.

The river "displayed a succession of the most beautiful scenery I had ever beheld…This magnificent theatre of nature has all the decorations which the trees and animals of the country can afford it.…The whole country displayed an exuberant verdure; the trees that bear a blossom were advancing fast to that delightful appearance, and the velvet rind of their branches reflecting the oblique rays of a rise or setting sun, added a splendid gaiety to the scene, which no expressions of mine are qualified to describe."[32]

The inadequacy of language struck Mackenzie again on his return from the Pacific. Reflecting on their "homeward journey," Mackenzie and his companions gazed out on the scene before them. He wrote: "Such was the depth of the precipices below, and the height of the mountains above, with the rude and wild magnificence of the scenery around, that I shall not attempt to describe such an astonishing and awful combination of objects; of which, indeed, no description can convey an adequate idea."[33]

Mackenzie revisited this theme at the conclusion of his account. Returning to the fort from which he had commenced his voyage, he observed: "Here my voyages of discovery terminate. Their toils and their dangers, their solicitudes and sufferings, have not been exaggerated in my description. On the contrary, in many instances, language has failed me in the attempt to describe them." Lewis, thus, could only have been helped in the conceptualization of his encounter with the sublime by borrowing the literary device that Mackenzie employed routinely.[34]

Likewise, there are experiences in Mackenzie's *Voyages* that clearly prefigure the now near mythic story of Lewis at Lemhi Pass. Reporting on the geographical information supposedly provided by Shoshone Chief Cameahwait about the country west of the divide, Lewis said the "information fell far short of my expectations or wishes." The Salmon River to the west "was obstructed by sharp pointed rocks and the rapidity of the stream such that the whole surface of the river was beat into perfect foam as far as the eye could reach."[35]

Similarly, when Mackenzie had reached the Continental Divide at a more northerly intersection twelve years earlier, he heard reports that "could not be more unfavourable or discouraging." Eventually Mackenzie, like Lewis and Clark years later, was convinced, based on Indian information, of the advisability of abandoning the dream of a quick river descent to the ocean and proceeded overland instead.[36]

As for Lewis's famed story of the Shoshone "fraturnal" or "national hug," Mackenzie experienced a remarkably similar gesture. On his final push to Pacific tidewater, Mackenzie came to what he called the Great Village. He started his greeting by shaking hands, but soon a succession of villagers took him serially in their arms. "These embraces," Mackenzie related, "which at first rather surprised me, I soon found to be marks of regard and friendship." At this village, Mackenzie's flattering reception was capped by the chief presenting "a very handsome robe of a sea-otter skin, which he had on, and covered me with." This scene, of course, is more than a little reminiscent of the storied episode in Lewis and Clark lore of Cameahwait adorning Lewis with his tippet, an object Lewis prized so much that he had his portrait drawn wearing it.[37]

Lewis also appears to have studied Mackenzie's stratagem of securing Indian support of the expedition in the short term with promises of trade in the long run. Mackenzie once told a group of Native people that if they helped him at that moment, he would either return himself "or send others to them, with such articles as they appeared to want: particularly arms and ammunition, with which they would be able to prevent their enemies from invading them."[38]

Correspondingly, Lewis told Cameahwait that after the expedition returned to their home "towards the rising sun whitemen would come to them with an abundance of guns and every other article necessary to their defence and comfort, and that they would be enabled to supply themselves with these articles on reasonable terms." The Shoshones, Lewis stated, "expressed great pleasure at this information and said they had been long anxious to see the whitemen that traded guns; and that we might rest assured of their friendship and that they would do whatever we wished them."[39]

Lewis's Lemhi script follows Mackenzie's discourse with remarkable fidelity. When Lewis returned to the Missouri side of the divide with Cameahwait and a band of Shoshones to meet Clark and the rest of the party, he took the opportunity to report that "every article about us appeared to excite astonishment in their minds." This is reminiscent of the episode when Mackenzie crossed the divide and found himself on the upper reaches of what would later be named the Fraser River, recording that the resident Indians observed "every thing about us, with a mixture of admiration and astonishment." Lewis remarked that even the "sagacity" of Seaman was admired, using the same favored descriptor that Mackenzie had employed for his canine companion.[40]

As the expedition proceeded west, its next great achievement was the difficult traverse of the Lolo Trail. On September 22, 1805, as Lewis's trailing party emerged from the Bitterroot Mountains onto Weippe Prairie, he penned the last memorable passage he would write until sequestered at Fort Clatsop the following winter: "The pleasure I now felt in having tryumphed over the rocky Mountains and descending once more to a level and fertile country where there was every rational hope of finding a comfortable subsistence for myself and [the] party can be more readily conceived than expressed, nor was the flattering prospect of the final success of the expedition less pleasing."[41]

Much as he did before leaving Fort Mandan, on this occasion Lewis had days if not weeks to anticipate his narrative requirements, and once again he relied on Mackenzie for inspiration. Describing a state of expeditionary affairs as "more readily conceived than expressed" was a favored rhetorical device of Mackenzie's in situations in which his party emerged from difficult circumstances, such as the Peace River canyon portage or the frustration of having to end their river voyage and proceed west overland. At an exploratory junction parallel to Lewis's situation on Weippe Prairie above the Clearwater River, which promised a passage to the Pacific, Mackenzie's party anticipated "the pleasure they should enjoy in getting clear of their present difficulties and gliding onwards with a strong and steady stream." Like Lewis, Mackenzie wrote of "the inexpressible satisfaction of finding" himself "on the West side of the…mountains."[42]

Because Lewis ceased writing at the Nez Perce villages, continuing from there westward to Fort Clatsop, Clark's account provides the principal voice of the expedition's concluding leg to its terminus at the ocean. But as noted earlier, Clark was also a close student of *Voyages from Montreal*. Clark did not seek recourse to Mackenzie as often as the intermittently indolent Lewis because the latter had the additional pressure of responding to the narrative standard set in *Voyages*, but when pressed by exploratory exigency for narrative text Clark also relied on the Scotsman. When the American captains reached the great forks of the Columbia on October 16, 1805, Mackenzie was on their mind. Given the relative size of the two forks, to their surprise it appeared Mackenzie had been on the main stem of the river while their course down what came to be known as the Snake River was a junior tributary. Clark wrote a short ethnographic note detailing Native body type and stature, head flattening, ornamentation, and respect for tribal elders that was a virtual copy of what Mackenzie had written when he (mistakenly) concluded that he had reached the Columbia River at a more northerly point.[43]

Of course, Lewis resumed his journal keeping by the time the return voyage began in earnest, and there we find yet another instance where the voice of Mackenzie resonates in Lewis's account. In June 1806, Lewis concluded that it would be "madness" to proceed through the snow-choked Bitterroots without a guide. Accordingly, the detachment returned to the Weippe Prairie—a retreat that Lewis mistakenly determined was the first "retrograde march" the expedition had been compelled to make. In describing the mood in camp that night, Lewis said, "the party were a good deel dejected tho' not so as I had apprehended they would have been." Apprehended—which is to say, learned—how and from whom?[44]

Thirteen years earlier, Mackenzie had reluctantly concluded that his voyage down what he believed to be the Columbia could not proceed farther. Worse, Mackenzie and his men had to retrace a considerable distance of their previous course in order to hit the jumping-off point for the trail that would eventually lead them to the ocean at Bella Coola. Mackenzie was distressed at this turn of events because, as he wrote, "in a voyage of this kind, a retrograde motion could not fail to cool the ardour, slacken the zeal, and weaken the confidence of those, who have no greater inducement in the undertaking, than to follow the conductor of it."[45]

Students of the American expedition know that the stories of Mackenzie and Lewis crossed again after the expedition in publisher David McKeehan's acid critique of the latter's ego and accomplishments. Defending the right of his client, Sergeant Patrick Gass, to publish what Lewis considered an unauthorized account of the expedition, McKeehan asserted that many facets of Lewis's "darling project" had been exaggerated. McKeehan published his complaint as an open letter to Lewis in a Pittsburgh newspaper on April 14, 1807, occupying an entire page of print. Of the several streams of McKeehan's thoughts, what most interests us here are his observations on the one point that was touted with great fanfare during the recent bicentennial era, at least in the most popular accounts of Ambrose and filmmaker Ken Burns—"the hazardous nature of the enterprize and the courage necessary for undertaking it."[46]

McKeehan stated: "Mr. M'Kenzie with a party consisting of about one fourth part of the number under your command, with means which will not bear a comparison with those furnished you, and without the *authority,* the *flags,* or *medals* of his government, crossed the Rocky mountains several degrees north of your rout, and for the *first time* penetrated to the Pacific Ocean." (Emphasis is from the original.) The mocking continued; indeed, it dug deeper. "You had the advantage of the information contained in his journal, and could in some degree estimate and guard against the dangers and difficulties you were to meet."[47] McKeehan's barrage must have truly stung Lewis and it may have been another contributing factor in Lewis's ultimate failure to produce an expedition narrative.

In contrast to the thirty-three members that formed the permanent party in Lewis and Clark's expedition, Mackenzie's entourage in 1793 consisted of nine men: six French Canadian voyageurs (two of whom had been on the expedition to the Arctic four years before); two Native guide interpreters; and a second-in-command, Alexander McKay. Not as formidable a figure as Clark, McKay was a more than able assistant who later figured in another famed chapter in Northwest history, going down with the *Tonquin* at Clayoquot Sound on the west coast of Vancouver Island in 1811. Altogether, Mackenzie's team averaged a vigorous twenty miles of travel a day through the Canadian wilderness.[48]

The curious aspect of McKeehan's commentary is that the insight about the value of Mackenzie's account could have come only from Sergeant Gass himself. Another, even stronger, clue to the ubiquity of Mackenzie's *Voyages* as a handbook is found in the journal composed by one of the more junior members of the Lewis and Clark party, Private Joseph Whitehouse. In the preface to the fair copy of Whitehouse's original notebook, the erstwhile enlisted man noted that during the voyage he "furnished" himself "with books, and also got from Captains Lewis and Clark, every information that lay in their power in order to compleat and make [his] Journal correct."[49] This revealing passage gives us a rare insight into one of the most important aspects of the expedition's operations—the composition of the journals. The clear implication to be drawn from Whitehouse is that the traveling library was frequently referred to and, as Gass and McKeehan more than hinted, no book was employed more regularly than Mackenzie's *Voyages*.

In one notable instance, Whitehouse outdid his commanders' penchant for Mackenzian phrasing. At the conclusion of his prefatory comments in the fair copy of his journal, Whitehouse plagiarized an entire paragraph from Mackenzie's narrative. In the preface to his book, Mackenzie wrote: "I am not a candidate for literary fame: at the same time, I cannot but indulge the hope that this volume, with all its imperfections, will not be thought unworthy the attention of the scientific geographer; and that, by unfolding countries hitherto unexplored, and which, I presume, may now be considered as part of the British dominions, it will be received as a faithful tribute to the prosperity of my country." Whitehouse used all of the above words, except for substituting "as a part belonging to the United States" for "as part of the British dominions."[50] Internal documentary evidence shows that the expedition's journal keepers frequently borrowed from each other around the campfire but they sought recourse to Mackenzie almost as often.

Mackenzie himself could never know how important his narrative was to the creation of the Lewis and Clark record. But the Scotsman's intuition about the Americans did not fail him. Provoked by press reports about the return of Lewis and Clark, and perhaps in response to Lewis's letter warning the public about unauthorized accounts (the same instrument that riled McKeehan),[51] Mackenzie issued his only known comment about the American expedition in March 1808. In his letter to Viscount Castlereagh, the British secretary of state for war and the colonies, Mackenzie took his own turn at belittling the American accomplishment. Advising Castlereagh on the imperial consequences of Lewis and Clark's venture, Mackenzie wrote:

> It being evident from the exertions of the American Government, that it is their intention to claim under the right of Discoveries of Captains Lewis and Clark, who, it is said, have traversed the Country by Land and Water from the Missisipi to the Pacific Ocean exclusive Privileges to the intermediate Country, as well as to the Coast Northward from the Spanish Boundary to the Latitude of 50, but these Pretensions may be resisted on the following grounds; that if they found their Claims on Discovery, it is notoriously groundless in the first Place—as to the North West Coast, because the whole of it had been visited by Great Britain, and other nations, and settlements made in some Parts, long before the United States of America existed as a Nation and lately by this Country [Great Britain] at Nootka, being before they acquired Louisiana, or fitted out the expedition of Discovery under Captains Lewis and Clark; and, in the second Place, as to the intermediate Territory: because I myself, known to have been the first, who crossed thro' it to the Columbia, and from the Columbia to the Pacific Ocean in the year 1793.[52]

It is frequently averred—indeed, it has become an axiom of Lewis and Clark studies—that Lewis never prepared a line of copy intended to form the narrative of his expedition. This is mistaken on two counts. First, most if not all of Lewis's account of the voyage up the Missouri from Fort Mandan to Lemhi Pass appears to be a draft of text intended for publication and not a record of proceedings made in the field. Second, and perhaps more directly, there is the matter of Lewis's "Essay on an Indian Policy," which appeared in an inconclusive and truncated form as an appendix to the edition of the Lewis and Clark journals paraphrased by Biddle in 1814.[53]

To the modern eye, the attachment of Lewis's essay seems oddly intrusive, because it has no apparent connection to the course of events just described by Biddle. However, the fact that Biddle included it suggests that Clark or Jefferson may have encouraged him to do so because they knew of their deceased friend's intention for this narrative, one that makes sense only within the Mackenzian paradigm that was Lewis's narrative milieu.

As a draft policy statement, Lewis's essay is an obvious rejoinder to the concluding few paragraphs of Mackenzie's *Voyages* and could well have been an indication of the larger narrative Lewis intended to publish. In this addendum, Lewis issues a challenge to his government every bit as vehement as the fur merchant did to his British superiors in the concluding paragraphs of *Voyages from Montreal*. Lewis's serial recommendations constituted a strategy distinctly aimed at thwarting the British on the upper Missouri. Lewis asked: "Can we begin the work of exclusion too soon?" If the United States did not exclude the British forthwith, Lewis predicted, "no such attempts will ever be made, and, consequently…we shall for several generations be taxed with the defence of a country which to us would be no more than a barren waste." (A waste because the British would have trapped out the country of its commercially valuable peltries.)[54]

That Mackenzie's North West Company was underselling the American competition on the upper Missouri rankled Lewis. In addition to the active exclusion of the British, Lewis advocated such countermeasures as the formation of a series of posts on the Missouri from which Indian agents for the American government and other guards could enforce licensing regulations, like the prohibition of alcohol. In short, Lewis argued, the United States needed a more forthright commercial policy "in order to contravene the machinations by the Northwest company for practice in that quarter." Turning Mackenzie's epithet "adventurers" into a virtue, Lewis stated, "if the American merchant does not adventure, the field is at once abandoned to the Northwest company."[55]

In this manner, Lewis, in his last major pronouncement about the West before his death, concludes his own story by taking it back precisely to the origins of the expedition. In his very last paragraph in *Voyages*, Mackenzie spoke of the "many political reasons" guiding his mind on the matter of expanding Great Britain's commercial prospects. Surely Lewis in his essay was working in the same mercantilist idiom. From the beginning of his western venture to the end, Lewis was seemingly under Mackenzie's influence. The Scotsman was nearly as constant a companion to Lewis before, during, and after his "darling project" as Clark had been.[56]

———————— NOTES ————————

1. Harry Fritz made the suggestion in Linda Juneau and David Purviance, ed., "Native Voices: The New Lewis and Clark," in *A Confluence of Cultures: Native Americans and the Expedition of Lewis and Clark* (Missoula: University of Montana, 2003), 62–63; Barry Gough, *First across the Continent: Sir Alexander Mackenzie* (Norman: University of Oklahoma Press, 1997), xviii, 3. For another article on Mackenzie's influence on the American explorers, see Barbara Belyea, "Heroes and Hero Worship," *Oregon Humanities* (Spring 2004): 38–43; Alexander Mackenzie, *Voyages From Montreal, on the River St. Laurence, through the Continent of North America, to the Frozen and Pacific Oceans, in the Years 1789 and 1793* (London, 1801). Specific citations herein to Mackenzie's *Voyages* are from the version prepared by W. Kaye Lamb, ed., *The Journals and Letters of Sir Alexander Mackenzie* (London, Cambridge University Press, 1970).

2. Gary E. Moulton, ed., *The Journals of the Lewis & Clark Expedition* (Lincoln: University of Nebraska Press, 1983–2001), 6: 60–61. Hereafter cited as Moulton, *Journals*, followed by the volume and page number(s). Readers who are not familiar with the Lewis and Clark story should note that I have adopted the custom in the study of the captains to maintain all but the most grotesque misspellings. Most commonly, as in this case, the lack of conformed spelling was a particular challenge for William Clark. However great he was as an explorer, he was no grammarian.

3. Moulton, *Journals*, 6: 52, 61–62, 66; 1: maps 89, 91.

4. Clark's draft map denotes the location of this tree with the initials *WC* and *ML*. Moulton, *Journals*, 1: map 91; 6: 66, 107; William H. Goetzmann, *New Lands, New Men: America and the Second Great Age of Discovery* (New York: Viking, 1986), 111, 114.

5. Goetzmann, *New Lands*, 114.

6. Moulton, *Journals*, 2: 3; John Logan Allen, *Lewis and Clark and the Image of the American Northwest* (New York: Dover, 1991), 63; Stephen E. Ambrose, *Undaunted Courage: Meriwether Lewis, Thomas Jefferson, and the Opening of the American West* (New York: Simon and Schuster, 1996), 74–76; Goetzmann, 112; Derek Hayes, *First Crossing: Alexander Mackenzie, His Expedition across North America, and the Opening of the Continent* (Seattle: Sasquatch Books, 2001), 114, 256; James P. Ronda, *Lewis and Clark among the Indians* (Lincoln: University of Nebraska Press, 1984), 1; Lamb, *Mackenzie Journals*, 417.

7. Lamb, *Mackenzie Journals*, 418.

8. Stephen Dow Beckham et al., *The Literature of the Lewis and Clark Expedition: A Bibliography and Essays* (Portland, OR: Lewis & Clark College, 2003), 36, 53; Lamb, *Mackenzie Journals*, 107; Belyea, "Heroes," 39.

9. Moulton, *Journals*, 7: 10; Lamb, *Mackenzie Journals*, 370.

10. Lamb, *Mackenzie Journals*, 266, 302, 372, 389, 406; Moulton, *Journals*, 2: 79, 82; 4: 66, 85, 113, 336, 383, 411; 5: 112.

11. Lamb, *Mackenzie Journals*, 239, 359; Elliott Coues, ed., *History of the Expedition under the Command of Lewis and Clark* (New York: F.P. Harper, 1893), 2: 702, 710, 720. The Coues book is an annotated version of the edition paraphrased by Biddle: Meriwether Lewis, *History of the Expedition under the Command of Captains Lewis and Clark...* (Philadelphia, 1814). On the change of clothes, see Rex Ziak, *In Full View: A True and Accurate Account of Lewis and Clark's Arrival at the Pacific Ocean, and Their Search for a Winter Camp along the Lower Columbia River* (Astoria, OR: Moffitt House Press, 2002), 9.

12. Hayes, *First Crossing*, 113, 212–14, 218, 220; Lamb, *Mackenzie Journals*, 378.

13. Moulton, *Journals*, 4: 259, 304; 5: 164; 6: 66, 70, 72, 81, 107; 8: 181, 184, 225, 237.

14. Ambrose, *Undaunted Courage*, 75; Thomas P. Slaughter, *Exploring Lewis and Clark: Reflections on Men and Wilderness* (New York: Alfred A. Knopf, 2003), 41. Lewis could hardly have been surprised that another explorer beat him to his discovery zone since he viewed Vancouver's maps in Philadelphia while preparing for the expedition. See Donald Jackson, *Letters of the Lewis and Clark Expedition with Related Documents: 1783–1854* (Urbana: University of Illinois Press, 1978), 1: 53.

15. Allen, *Lewis and Clark*, 131; Goetzmann, *New Lands*, 114.

16. Beckham, *Literature of the Lewis and Clark*, 36; Percy G. Adams, *Travelers and Travel Liars, 1660–1800* (Berkeley: University of California, 1962), 11, 84–85, 142–61 passim, 229.

17. Lamb, *Mackenzie Journals*, 34–35, 59.

18. Hayes, *First Crossing*, 254.

19. Slaughter, *Exploring Lewis and Clark*, 32.

20. Moulton, *Journals*, 4: 9–10.

21. Ibid., 4: 12n1; Lamb, *Mackenzie Journals*, 328.

22. Moulton, *Journals*, 4: 9, 14; 5: 128, 131n6, 249, 250n2, 339; 7: 248.

23. Hayes, *First Crossing*, 93, 113; Lamb, *Mackenzie Journals*, 314, 317, 337, 340.

24. Moulton, *Journals*, 4: 270–71.

25. Lamb, *Mackenzie Journals*, 200, 201; Hayes, *First Crossing*, 112. Mackenzie had actually reached the ocean by the time of this incident, but had not yet realized that fact. Lamb, *Mackenzie Journals*, 201n1.

26. Lamb, *Mackenzie Journals*, 279; Moulton, *Journals*, 4: 270–71.

27. Lamb, *Mackenzie Journals*, 323–24.

28. Moulton, *Journals*, 4: 284–85.

29. Ibid., 290.

30. Lamb, *Mackenzie Journals*, 128; Moulton, *Journals*, 4: 290.

31. Moulton, *Journals*, 4: 285.

32. Lamb, *Mackenzie Journals*, 258–59.

33. Ibid., 395.

34. Ibid., 407.

35. Moulton, *Journals*, 5: 88.

36. Lamb, *Mackenzie Journals*, 300, 321.

37. Moulton, *Journals*, 5: 79, 104, 109; Lamb, *Mackenzie Journals*, 365; Carolyn Ives Gilman, *Lewis and Clark: Across the Divide* (Washington, DC: Smithsonian Institution Press, 2003), 198.

38. Lamb, *Mackenzie Journals*, 315.

39. Moulton, *Journals*, 5: 91–92.

40. Ibid., 112; Lamb, *Mackenzie Journals*, 313, 389.

41. Moulton, *Journals*, 5: 229.

42. Lamb, *Mackenzie Journals*, 273, 301, 303, 321.
43. For a broader exploration of this episode, including Mackenzie's influence on Lewis and Clark's perception of the Columbia watershed, see David L. Nicandri, *River of Promise: Lewis and Clark on the Columbia* (Bismarck, ND: Dakota Institute Press, 2009), 97–103.
44. Moulton, *Journals*, 8: 31–32. Lewis and Clark reversed course several times in rounding "Point Distress" (today's Point Ellice) in November 1805. See Moulton, *Journals*, 6: 39, 43, 48; Ziak, *In Full View*, 11, 23–25, 39, 53.
45. Lamb, *Mackenzie Journals*, 321–22.
46. Jackson, *Letters*, 2: 399–408 (McKeehan quoted on page 401); Slaughter, *Exploring Lewis and Clark*, 215n7.
47. Jackson, *Letters*, 2: 401–22.
48. Gough, *First across the Continent*, 123; Lamb, *Mackenzie Journals*, 21–22.
49. Moulton, *Journals*, 11: 6.
50. Lamb, *Mackenzie Journals* 59–60; Moulton, *Journals*, 11: 7. The Whitehouse fair copy is written in the hand of someone other than Whitehouse (Ibid., xvi).
51. See Jackson, *Letters*, 2: 385–86, 386n, for a history of the Lewis-McKeehan exchange.
52. Lamb, *Mackenzie Journals*, 518–19. Of course, herein Mackenzie mistook the Columbia River for the Fraser, after whom the stream was eventually named by virtue of Simon Fraser's expedition in the same year Mackenzie was responding to Lewis. (Ibid., 22).
53. On the edited nature of the journals of Lewis and Clark, see Slaughter, *Exploring Lewis and Clark*, 32–33. For an excellent analysis of the distinctions between "campfire journals" and texts that filter the accounts of the exploration for narrative effect, see Barbara Belyea, ed., *Columbia Journals: David Thompson*, reprint ed. (Seattle: University of Washington Press, 1998), ix, xvi, xvii, xxi. Lewis's essay can be found in Coues, 3: 1215–43, and in Reuben Gold Thwaites, ed., *Original Journals of the Lewis and Clark Expedition, 1804–1806* (New York, 1905), 7: 369–88 as "Lewis's Observations and Reflections on Upper Louisiana, 1809."
54. Thwaites, 7:377–78. Neither Jackson nor Moulton included Lewis's essay in their compilations, contributing to its obscurity.
55. Thwaites, 7: 379, 380, 382, 385, 388; Lamb, *Mackenzie Journals*, 418.
56. Lamb, *Mackenzie Journals*, 418.

Jefferson's Instructions, by Roger Cooke (2003). Courtesy of the Washington State Historical Society. WSHS 2005.22.3.

CHAPTER 3

THE RHYME OF THE GREAT NAVIGATOR:

THE LITERATURE OF CAPTAIN COOK AND ITS INFLUENCES ON THE JOURNALS OF LEWIS AND CLARK

James Cook's influence and prominence within what has been labeled the Second Great Age of Discovery was paramount. Indeed, he was the emblematic figure of Enlightenment-era exploration, having institutionalized the template for scientific discovery; this in contrast to the overtly imperialist orientation of the preceding era—what might be called the Age of Columbus. Thomas Jefferson borrowed from the British Admiralty's instructions to Cook, found in the published accounts of the renowned navigator's three great voyages of exploration to the Pacific (1768–80), to script his own to Meriwether Lewis. For the second and third of these ventures Cook largely drafted his own mission objectives, but his trips' impact transcended the mere tactical. To cite but one example, Cook's exploits heavily informed the narrative spine of the *Rime of the Ancient Mariner*, whose author, Samuel Taylor Coleridge, had been instructed by William Wales, the principal astronomer on Cook's second voyage.

As a practical matter, the explorer whose work was most often and explicitly referenced in the journals of Lewis and Clark was George Vancouver. His expedition, 1792–94, commonly misunderstood as a voyage to look for what Cook missed, was actually a more nuanced search for a second-generation Northwest Passage. Samuel Hearne had eliminated the possibility of a subarctic saltwater passage from the Atlantic to the Pacific in 1771–72, a finding which drove Cook to even higher latitudes. That quest was thwarted by ice in 1778 so, given the durability of the Northwest Passage as a cartographic image, Vancouver was dispatched to look for an inland extension of the Pacific that was an analogue to Hudson Bay—a sea that, with a bridge of land between them, shortened the distance between the two oceans. Vancouver spent his first year of formal exploration—the late spring and summer of 1792—in the more southerly range of latitudes he was tasked to survey (basically the 40s), the area visited a decade later by Lewis and Clark. The key development intersecting with Lewis and Clark was Lieutenant William Broughton's exploration of the lower Columbia in the fall of 1792. Though Broughton's chart of the lower Columbia and its key place names (Mounts Hood and St. Helens) made Vancouver's expedition more immediate, Lewis and Clark were still mindful of Cook. This is most clearly evident in the first of two substantive and explicit references to Cook-related text found in the journals of the American captains, as well as a third one, secreted in Lewis's midcontinent grandiloquence at the Great Falls of the Missouri.

Cook's search for the Northwest Passage did not begin, strictly speaking, until he had been under sail for nearly two years, having made a passage to Cape Town, New Zealand, Tahiti, Hawaii, and Nootka; all that travel merely set the stage for the actual mission. In the same sense, Lewis and Clark did not commence the process of real discovery until they departed Fort Mandan for points west, a year and three-quarters after Lewis left Jefferson's company in Washington, DC. On the occasion of their jumping off onto the waters of the upper Missouri on April 7, 1805, Lewis penned a paragraph that is among the two or three most memorable or at least most oft-cited by historians. He wrote: "Our vessels consisted of six small canoes, and two large perogues. This little fleet, altho' not quite so rispectable as those of Columbus or Capt. Cook were still viewed by us with as much pleasure as those deservedly famed adventurers ever beheld theirs; and I dare say with quite as much anxiety for their safety and preservation."[1]

And with that, Lewis with Clark started their western quest, a variation on the same theme that had prompted Cook to come out of retirement to conduct his final voyage. In a sense, Lewis and Clark sought the *third* version of the Northwest Passage to evolve within a quarter century: their mission was to find an interlocking river system that would cross the continent, a route replacing both the classic saltwater corridor Cook was looking for or the intermediating midcontinental sea stretching toward Hudson Bay that Vancouver sought. This newest vision was first propagated and popularized by Alexander Mackenzie in his *Voyages from Montreal*, published in 1801, the true spring from which the Lewis and Clark Expedition welled up.

In some respects Lewis's invocation of the "fleets" of these great navigators is narrative whimsy. The reference to Cook, in particular, seems to be an attempt to burnish his project's stature since the great navigator's exploits were still in the working memory of geographers, whether of the armchair or practical variety. Richard Van Orman has made a similar claim, saying that Lewis wrote his departing text as a confidence-building exercise.[2] To be sure, Lewis's rhetorical reference to these two famous mariners, among the many he might have chosen, showed historical awareness. Each had inaugurated an entire age of discovery: in Columbus's case, of new continents, in Cook's, new oceanic pathways to, through, or around these new lands. Lewis's Dakota springtime reverie made for great copy in his journal, as evidenced by its appeal over the last two centuries, and almost certainly would have been included in his official account, had he published one. In any event, Columbus disappears from Lewis's text after this formulaic tribute, but Cook reappears in Clark's journal almost a year later, in a mysterious way.

Lewis's lines about his predecessor's fleets soar as exploratory literature, which is why they are so well known. The later entry by Clark is characteristically prosaic and therefore easy to miss but it actually allows us to probe more deeply into the dynamics that inform the creation of travel literature. Near modern Knappa, Oregon, during the second day after leaving Fort Clatsop on the voyage home, the captains came upon a Cathlamet Indian village. Lewis had already been keeping a journal at this point, so it is therefore novel that Clark (seemingly) records an observation on his own, rather than make a copy of Lewis's remarks as he often did when his counterpart was writing. Clark wrote of seeing "two very large elegant Canoes inlaid with Shills, those Shills I took to be teeth at first View, and the natives informed Several of the men that they [were] the teeth of their enemies which they had killed in War. [I]n examineing of them Closely haveing taken out Several pi[e]ces, we found that [they] were Sea Shells...[and] they also deckerate their Smaller wooden vessles with those Shells which have much the appearance of humane teeth[.] Capt Cook may have mistaken those Shills verry well for humane teeth without a Close examination."[3]

The Cathlamets were probably trying to enhance their martial stature with the story about their enemies' teeth. Then too, it may have been a joke. The plural "we" that discerned the truth of the decorative shells indicates that this was a group discussion, one that probably included Lewis. Given the larger volume of ethnographic content in Lewis's journals, he never addressed the matter. All we have to work with is Clark's note.

Any reference to Cook, especially to a supposed mistake the great navigator may have made, was sure to elicit Gary E. Moulton's attention in his annotation of the modern edition of Lewis and Clark's journals. Moulton looked at several facets of Clark's remark. He noted that the published account of Cook's third voyage was in Jefferson's library. Since Jefferson had a copy of Cook's narrative, Moulton plausibly reasoned that "Lewis was undoubtedly familiar with at least the portions treating the Northwest Coast of North America."[4] As outlined in this essay, I believe that Lewis was probably familiar with the entire three-voyage Cook oeuvre including, without question, the last two accounts. Here I refer not only to the official publications issued under the Admiralty's auspices, but also ancillary accounts such as those authored by second-voyage naturalists Johann Reinhold Forster and his son George Forster, plus that of Marine Corporal John Ledyard, the American seaman who rushed an unauthorized report of Cook's third voyage into print in 1782. These books would have been in either Jefferson's possession or in the library of the American Philosophical Society (APS) in Philadelphia where Lewis conducted his preparatory studies in 1803.

Moulton made a point to note that it was Clark, not Lewis, who made the observation about the canoes' decoration. Since Clark deviated from what is commonly referred to as his verbatim mode of journal keeping when Lewis was writing, a question arises: how to explain this departure from the norm, even if it is in reference, as Moulton said, "to a minor point in Cook's journals"?[5] The decoration of the Cathlamet canoes does indeed seem like something Lewis would pay attention to, not only because of his natural scholarly inclination and the division of labor between the captains, but especially because it is extremely unlikely Clark would have seen Cook's account out on the Kentucky frontier. This is not a criticism of Clark, his education, or his abilities. Lewis may have been the expedition's de facto ethnologist, but in terms of the practical management of human relations across the racial divide Clark was far better equipped than Lewis.

In order to shed further light on this episode, Moulton scrutinized John C. Beaglehole's edition of Cook's journals. There, Moulton discerned that although the Natives encountered at Nootka Sound (the indigenous settlement visited by Cook that was closest to Lewis and Clark's position on the lower Columbia) traded in human skulls and hands, Cook never recorded any reference "to human teeth as ornaments of canoes." Moulton implies that Clark's mistaken "impression" was perhaps derived from a misreading of Cook, a premise that also conveniently reinforces the orthodox understanding that Clark was quick to jump to conclusions; this as opposed to the supposedly more studied manner of the more scholarly Lewis. To explain Clark's sudden and unexpected interest in and knowledge of Cook, Moulton states that "it may have been Lewis who mentioned it to him."[6]

Alternatively and in conclusion, Moulton posits the John Ledyard theory. After circumnavigating the world by sail on Cook's third voyage, Ledyard later set upon the spectacular notion of a global circumambulation, in the most expansive understanding of that term. After crossing Siberia by carriage (which he nearly accomplished before being expelled by Empress Catherine II), Ledyard planned to transect the Bering Strait (whose narrowness Cook had first mapped) and from there hitch a ride to Nootka or some more southerly latitude with one of the Pacific maritime fur traders who followed in Cook's wake. Thence Ledyard imagined walking across North America with a canine companion to the Atlantic shore. Ledyard met Jefferson in Paris in 1785 while laying the groundwork for this ill-fated venture. From that circumstance Moulton theorized that Ledyard passed the decorative insight about canoes to Jefferson, who, decades later, conveyed it to Lewis verbally.

These implausible scenarios were dictated by a documentary problem, for, as Moulton correctly observed, the comment Clark presumed to correct "did not find its way into the published accounts" of Cook's voyage, including Ledyard's.[7] And that is where editor Moulton left it, somewhat inconclusively. I made this perplexing issue a sidebar project as part of my investigation of Cook, his high-latitude voyaging, and the evolution of the image of the Northwest Passage. What follows is the ethnographic context and origin of the story of human teeth decorating northwestern Native canoes. In addition, I track its convoluted route into the pages of Clark's journal, one that bypasses Ledyard, Jefferson, and Cook and courses instead through two other explorers unnamed by Clark.

As pointed out in the previous chapter and intermittently in my book *River of Promise*, North West Company fur trader and explorer Alexander Mackenzie loomed over the western third of Lewis and Clark's trek to the Pacific.[8] Though never formally acknowledged by Lewis or Clark for his contributions to their efforts, Mackenzie's *Voyages from Montreal* served as a veritable trail guide for the American captains. Many key tactics were initially modeled by Mackenzie and several noteworthy phrases, indeed whole paragraphs, were plagiarized by the captains from the Scotsman's account of his travels to the Arctic and the Pacific. In the main body of text describ-

ing his run to the Pacific tidewater in July 1793, Mackenzie notes, relative
to a Native canoe, that "the gunwale, fore and aft, was inlaid with the teeth
of the sea-otter." In a footnote to this text Mackenzie added (gratuitously
it turns out) an elaboration that gets to the heart of our concern: "As Captain Cooke has mentioned, that the people of the sea-coast adorned their
canoes with human teeth, I was more particular in my inquiries; the result
of which was, the most satisfactory proof, that he was mistaken: but his
mistake arose from the very great resemblance there is between human
teeth and those of the sea-otter."[9] Thus we see that Clark slyly appropriated Mackenzie's supposed insight about Cook's "mistake," but kept the
origination of this information hidden. But proving Mackenzie was Clark's
secret source begs the now transposed question: what information was
Mackenzie drawing on which allowed him to presume to criticize Cook?

Before commencing that investigation, a discursive qualification on
sources and the dynamics surrounding the creation of exploration texts.
Since Cook died on the third voyage, technically he was not the author

Best canoe navigators, by Roger Cooke (2003). A Chinook canoe leaves the Lewis and Clark
party in stunned amazement at Dismal Nitch as they head across a tumultuous Columbia
River. Clark deemed them "the best Canoe navigaters I ever Saw." Courtesy of the Washington State Historical Society. WSHS 2005.22.68.

of any published information detailing his last expedition. John Douglas was the editor of Cook's final report and though he certainly drew heavily on Cook's journal for the basic chronology and narrative flow (nigh to the captain's death), he supplemented it from time to time by recourse to journal copy provided by others. Most notable in this regard were the ethnological contributions of ship surgeon William Anderson and Lieutenant James King's cultural and geographical insights. On his own, King also authored the third and final volume of the official account that picks up the story after Cook's demise in February 1779, taking it to the conclusion of the voyage when the ships returned to Great Britain in the fall of 1780.

Douglas, as Cook's editor, had access to King's journal, including ethnographic observations recorded at Nootka in the spring of 1778. Therein, King made note of the arrival in the sound of some "Strangers" (a neighboring tribe) who had in their canoe a set of boxes that were "part of their household furniture" which were "ornament'd with bones & teeth indent'd."[10] Subsequently, in volume 2 of Cook's third-voyage account, Douglas expanded King's note by including a description of these boxes, which the tribes used to store armaments, masks, and other valuables. They were "often painted black, studded with the teeth of different *animals*, [emphasis added] or carved with a kind of freeze-work [*sic*], and figures of birds or animals, as decorations."[11] Several pages later, the "Cook" persona (in reality Douglas) adds a comment that some canoes in Nootka Sound "have a little carving, and are decorated by setting *seals* [emphasis added] teeth on the surface, like studs; as is the practice on their masks and weapons."[12] Since King's journal makes no such note, Douglas either gleaned this insight from Anderson's (still largely unpublished) journal or King mentioned it to him when reviewing the manuscript in advance of its publication in 1784. Nevertheless, the problem remains: Cook's published account, and the original journals underlying that narrative, clearly identify the decorative material as animal in origin, not human, as Mackenzie's and Clark's versions have it.

So, having worked this problem as a reverse progression from Clark to Mackenzie to Cook et al., let's play it forward. Cook, who is really Douglas serving as editor for a syncretic Cook/King/Anderson persona, publishes information about canoes seen at Nootka Sound decorated with seal's teeth. Mackenzie, arriving at tidewater to the inside of Vancouver Island in 1793, correctly attributes this decorative motif to the teeth of sea otters, but charges Cook with having mistakenly determined that the ornamentation was of human origin. Clark, next in line and with Mackenzie's book open before him, repeats the notion of Cook's mistake about human teeth, but personally finds the decorative element to be constituted by sea shells. (The source of the divergence, of course, is that Clark is on the lower Columbia River, not the British Columbia coast.) Since Cook (per Douglas) never said anything about human teeth decorating Native canoes, this is proof positive that Clark was snared in a plagiarist's trap that Mackenzie inadvertently set.

But if Clark was deviously gullible, Mackenzie was simply sloppy. Mackenzie did not (indeed could not possibly) find the line of text attributed to Cook describing Native canoes decorated with human teeth for the same reason Moulton couldn't—it doesn't exist. It is actually found in John Meares's 1790 narrative of fur trading on the Northwest Coast. Meares had spent a season trading at Nootka Sound in September 1788 and his exploits were widely publicized. Indeed, strictly speaking, it was Meares's two publications, not Cook's presumed faults, that actually spurred the Vancouver expedition.

Meares reported that after he left the Northwest Coast for China, his associates that were left behind for further trading were perceived to have run afoul of Spanish territorial claims in the North Pacific. Spanish Captain Esteban José Martínez seized Meares's small fort at Nootka Sound in July 1789 and also imprisoned one of Meares's associates, James Colnett (who had sailed with Cook), taking him as a prisoner to Mexico. Meares learned of these developments the following December while in Macao and determined upon an immediate return to England, which he reached in April 1790, to seek redress. His *Memorial…to the House of Commons, May 13, 1790* inflamed British public opinion and almost led to war. In due course Spain capitulated to British insistence on the ability of its traders to conduct their operations along the Northwest Coast, but as a collateral function of the arrangement signed on October 28, 1790, Spain agreed to return Meares's property to an agent of the British Crown inside the confines of Nootka Sound.

Vancouver ended up being that delegate, but he was also given an exploratory mission. After the *Memorial*, Meares published *Voyages Made in the Years 1788 and 1789, from China to the North West Coast of America*. In this tome Meares gave full vent to the emergent opinion of all the maritime fur traders who had followed Cook to that quarter of the globe in the 1780s. This new geography of hope, seizing upon the complexity of the Northwest Coast that Cook had neither the time, inclination, nor commission to explore in 1778, postulated that any one or more of the numerous inlets the traders had found along this long broken coastline provided access deep into North America's continental interior. Vancouver was charged with finding what speculative geographers conflated into a shortcut to Hudson Bay. In the event, this new Northwest Passage was as fugitive a notion as the one Cook was sent to verify in the Arctic. But to the point of our story, in an ethnographic digression within his *Voyages*, Meares wrote the following line of text in regard to the Native craft he saw on the Northwest Coast: "Some of these canoes are polished and painted, or curiously studded with human teeth, particularly on the stern and the prow."[13] Mackenzie, writing his memoir more than a decade after Meares's narrative appeared, simply misattributed Meares's observation, making it Cook's. Clark was merely the not-so-innocent bystander.

Though this whole episode is, to repeat Moulton's stipulation, "a minor point" in content, it nevertheless reinforces several salient aspects surrounding the exploratory dynamic. First, we see the foundational aspect of Cook's narrative, the initial description of the northwestern quadrant of North America or, at least, its coastline. Second, we note that the Lewis and Clark experience did not take place on a *tabula rasa*, given their reliance on Mackenzie for matters large and small. Here, Clark's appropriation is a somewhat inconsequential "fact." But as noted earlier in this book, at other intersections in their journey Mackenzie was so important to the captains they copied him directly and at length and never with attribution. Ultimately, this episode further justifies the need for historians to be vigilant in their appreciation of the evolution of the exploratory narrative from field note to published account and the duty to read the documentary record in parallel form, much like biblical scholars study the synoptic gospels.

Having addressed and unpacked the origins of the two explicit references to Captain Cook found in the journals of Lewis and Clark, let us look at another example of how a celebrated discovery text drew upon a larger literature without its author acknowledging sources. I refer to Lewis's narrative reflection on his encounter with the sublime in the vicinity of the Great Falls of the Missouri in the summer of 1805, the only text more oft-quoted than the expedition's departure from Fort Mandan.

A more extensive passage than the description of the leave-taking of Fort Mandan, Lewis's Great Falls rhapsody is a literary classic, replete with colorful imagery and memorable turns of phrase describing the river's thunderous cataracts. The falls, which he reached on June 13, 1805, were, for Lewis, "the grandest sight I ever beheld." The "impetuous courant" broke

"into a perfect white foam which assumes a thousand forms in a moment."
He reveled in the billowing spray, rainbows, and other elements that added
"not a little to the beauty of this majestically grand senery." Competently
recording what he encountered, Lewis nevertheless felt compelled to dep-
recate his effort with this famous passage:

> after wrighting this imperfect discription I again viewed the falls and was so much
> disgusted with the imperfect idea which it conveyed of the scene that I determined
> to draw my pen across it and begin agin, but then reflected that I could not perhaps
> succeed better than pening the first impressions of the mind; I wished for the pencil
> of Salvator Rosa or the pen of Thompson [*sic*], that I might be enabled to give to
> the enlightened world some just idea of this truly magnifficent and sublimely grand
> object, which has from the commencement of time been concealed from the view
> of civilized man; but this was fruitless and vain.

The next day he walked to the upper falls and again stood in wonder
at the river water "dashing against the rocky bottom" creating "foaming
billows of great hight." Like he had the day before, Lewis repeated his
incantation for the presence of "a skillful painter" to record "the precise
immage" of this *"pleasingly beautifull"* waterfall.[14]

There are many literary tropes commonly found in Enlightenment-era
exploratory accounts, some of which were highlighted in the previous
chapter. The most common are (1) the commander's expression of confident leadership that the men respond to cheerfully and without a hint of
repining; (2) the productive response to fatigues and hardships; (3) cultural
metamorphosis as represented by an exchange of garments or names; (4)
disparate species of animals seemingly forming ad hoc alliances to either
entertain or torment explorers with their antics or threatening demeanor;
and perhaps most recognizably, (5) the one just recited—the imperfect
description rendered in an amateurish or incomplete manner. Within this
last, what has been termed the trope of ineffability, there are several vari-
ants. The most favored by Mackenzie and Lewis was the suggestive hint of
an impending difficulty, or in some instances a natural wonder, quickly followed by a textual sleight of hand diverting the reader away from a detailed
explanation that might otherwise be expected. Instead, readers were urged
to employ their own faculties and imagine the scene or situation that was,
the authors confidently presumed, "more readily conceived than expressed."
In the present case, the most noteworthy element is Lewis's specific invocation of Rosa and Thomson (the latter curiously misspelled by Lewis,
but explained below). The exotic nature of these obscure references makes

them stand out in sharp relief amid the many lines that express Lewis's rapturous gaze upon the Great Falls and contribute immensely to the literary prominence of his journal entry for June 13, 1805. The reference to Rosa and Thomson contributes much to the perception of Lewis as a man of the world, certainly the Enlightenment.

Salvator Rosa (1615–73) was an Italian artist who, along with Claude Lorrain, was one of the progenitors of the picturesque mode of painterly expression. This artistic tradition was not an empirical style sympathetic to the Enlightenment's scientific outlook, and for that reason Rosa's baroque allegories were much admired by and anticipated the form of nineteenth-century Romantics, such as the Hudson River School. In this

Gustav Sohon, *Great Falls of the Missouri River*, in *Narrative and Final Report of Explorations for a Route for a Pacific Railroad, Near the Forty-Seventh and Forty-Ninth Parallels of North Latitude from St. Paul to Puget Sound*, by Isaac I. Stevens (Washington, DC: Thomas H. Ford, 1860), opposite p. 183. This lithograph was the first published image of the Missouri's Great Falls derived from a sketch actually drawn in the field. Originally delineated by Sohon, a private in the US Army attached to the Pacific Railroad Survey of Isaac Stevens, 1853–55, the scene depicts the furthest downstream and largest cataract (falling 87 feet) of the five that Meriwether Lewis discovered in 1805. At the left margin of the image, Sohon captured a hint of the mist and sprays that Lewis's text described. Courtesy of the Washington State Historical Society. WSHS 2005.0.21.49.

sense, Lewis is properly seen as a transitional figure in the evolution of cultural projection. Born late in the Enlightenment and educated to its tenets, his mood often reflected the passionate outlook of the ensuing Romantic age. By comparison to the parallel vein of maritime exploration, the emotionally detached and laconic Cook contrasted with the moodiness of the *Bounty's* William Bligh and Fletcher Christian.

James Thomson (1700–48) was a well-known Scottish poet long since eclipsed in prominence by Robert Burns. Thomson seems to have been a favorite among educated young gentlemen, or, at least, it was fashionable to have presumed to read his poetry. He is best known for his paean to nature, *The Seasons*, which appeared serially starting with "Winter" in 1726. The complete four-part set, including the finale "Autumn," was first published in 1730. We do not know whether Cook read Thomson, but two gentlemen travelling with the great navigator on his second voyage did: Wales and George Forster. William Wales (1734–88), introduced earlier in this chapter as the mathematician and astronomer who was Coleridge's instructor, had observed the transit of Venus on Hudson Bay (while Cook drew the assignment in Tahiti). The Board of Longitude thereafter appointed Wales to accompany Cook's second voyage in search of *Terra Australis Incognita*. Besides monitoring the chronometers and related navigational duties, Wales taught Midshipman George Vancouver how to make proper astronomical observations.

Wales was thirty-seven when he left port with Cook, but George Forster (1754–94) was a mere seventeen years of age when he signed on as assistant naturalist and illustrator, serving his father Johann Reinhold Forster, who had taken over for Joseph Banks as the lead naturalist when the latter withdrew from the voyage. Both father and son published books in the immediate aftermath of Cook's second voyage. A close reading of the Cook record, including the works of the Forsters, shows that Lewis was inspired to refer to such exotic European figures as Rosa and Thomson by what he read in the Forsters' books. Thereby it also provides an analogue to the clever and sometimes devious borrowings Lewis and Clark made from Mackenzie as discussed earlier.

Recalling Lewis's tribute to the grandeur of the Great Falls of the Missouri, let us first consider Captain Cook's rare attempt at reaching for a description of the sublime. In February 1773, Cook terminated his first foray along the edge of the Antarctic ice sheet in the Indian Ocean's high latitudes. This was the end of the first southern summer of his second voyage. Having crossed the Antarctic Circle for the first time southeast of Cape Town earlier in the season, he considered making a second run across the line but ultimately determined against it, heading toward New Zealand for respite instead. His published account (issued after he had left on the third and final voyage) adapted language from his ship's log summarizing the ubiquity and danger associated with his encounters with great masses of field ice, or more memorably, tabular icebergs. The latter were often so immense that Cook and his compatriots frequently referred to them as ice islands, and the chunks they calved, tellingly, as ice rocks. Cook, no longer in the literary shadow of the absent Banks, initially focused on the risks associating with navigating in and around the ice islands, but then he turned to their attributes. Among these was their service as a supply of fresh water, but in a burst of melodramatic prose he hailed "their very romantic appearance, greatly heightened by the foaming and dashing of the waves into the curious holes and caverns which are formed in many of them; the whole exhibiting a view which at once filled the mind with admiration and horror, and can only be described by the hand of an able painter."[15]

Cook does not name Rosa here, but the mood, and the mode, had been set. Shortly thereafter, near the end of March 1773, the expedition made landfall at the southern tip of New Zealand. The expedition sailed into the fjord-like Dusky Bay (now Dusky Sound) and, after settling in, Cook, the Forsters, and the expedition artist William Hodges (1744–97) went in a small boat to observe the cataracts that poured into what they called "Cascade Cove." In his journal, Cook says Hodges's field sketch (later made into an oil painting) "exhibits at one view a better discription of it than I can give, huge heaps of stones lies at the foot of this Cascade which have been brought by the force of the Stream from adjacent mountains."[16]

This was an echo of Cook's ice island reflection, but both of the Forsters devoted far more eloquence to the scene in their publications. George Forster's book *A Voyage Round the World* was published first, in 1777, because his father's account, *Observations Made during a Voyage Round the World* (1778), was wrapped up in a dispute with the Admiralty over its relationship to Cook's forthcoming narrative. By preceding both Cook's and his father's publications, and describing what was contemporaneously saluted as the greatest exploratory voyage of all time, George Forster's account became one of the most influential narratives in the history of exploration. Expounding upon the wonders of Dusky Bay as they first sailed into it, Forster writes: "The view of rude sceneries in the style of *Rosa*, of antediluvian forests which cloathed the rock, and of numerous rills of water, which every where rolled down the steep declivity, altogether conspired to complete our joy."[17]

As noted above, the younger Forster was among those who later took the short boat trip with Cook to Cascade Cove. His description of this sojourn, a text remarkably similar to Lewis's narrative of his Great Falls tableau, reads as follows:

> We directed our course to the cove...which we had observed from afar a few days ago, and which had induced us to call this inlet Cascade Cove. This water-fall, at the distance of a mile and a half, seems to be but inconsiderable, on account of its great elevation; but after climbing about two hundred yards upwards, we obtained a full prospect of it, and found indeed a view of great beauty and grandeur before us. The first object which strikes the beholder, is a clear column of water, apparently eight [or] ten yards in circumference, which is projected with a great impetuosity from the perpendicular rock, at the height of one hundred yards. Nearly at the fourth part of the whole height, this column meeting a part of the same rock, which now acquires a little inclination, spreads on its broad back into a limpid sheet of about twenty-five yards in width. Here its surface is curled, and dashes upon every little eminence in its rapid descent, till it is all collected in a fine bason about sixty yards in circuit, included on three sides by the natural walls of the rocky chasm, and in front by huge masses of stone irregularly piled above each other. Between them the stream finds its way, and runs foaming with the greatest rapidity along the slope of the hill to sea. The whole neighbourhood of the cascade, to a distance of an hundred yards around, is filled with the steam or watery vapour formed by the violence of the fall. This mist however was so thick, that it penetrated our clothes in a few minutes, as effectively as a shower of rain would have done. We mounted on the highest stone before the bason, and looking down into it, were struck with the sight of a beautiful rainbow of a perfectly circular form, which was produced by the meridian rays of the sun refracted in the vapour of the cascade. Beyond this circle the rest of the steam was tinged with the prismatic colours refracted in an inverted order.... The noise of the cascade is so loud, and so repeatedly reverberated from the echoing rocks, that it drowns almost every other sound; the birds seemed to retire from it to a little distance, where the shrill notes of thrushes, the graver pipe of wattle-birds, and the enchanting melody of various creepers resounded on all sides, and completed the beauty of this wild and romantic spot. On turning round we beheld an extensive bay, strewed as it were with small islands, which are covered with lofty trees; beyond them on one side, the mountains rise majestic on the main land, capt with clouds and perpetual snow; and on the other, the immense ocean bounded our view. The grandeur of this scene was such, that the powers of description fall short of the force and beauty of nature, which could only be truly imitated by the pencil of Mr. Hodges, who went on this voyage with us; and whose performances do great credit and honour to his judgment and execution, as well as to the choice of his employers. Satisfied with the contemplation of this magnificent sight, we directed our attention next to the flowers which enlivened the ground, and the small birds which sung very cheerfully all round us.[18]

Cook scholars have long believed Johann Forster penned many passages in George's book, if not most of them. Regardless, whether prompted by his son's work or as originator in both publications, the elder Forster's ensuing discussion of the cascades in the fjord of Dusky Bay is also worth quoting:

> We observed, in the several inlets and arms forming this spacious bay, sometimes *cascades* rushing rapidly down, and falling from vast heights before they met with another rock. Some of these cascades with their neighbouring scenery, require the pencil and genius of a SALVATOR ROSA to do them justice: however the ingenious artist [Hodges], who went with us on this expedition has great merit, in having executed some of these romantic landscapes in a masterly manner.[19]

These passages from the Forsters surely represent what Lewis sought to emulate at the Great Falls and, in some particulars, reached. He assuredly did not copy the key phrases directly; for unlike Mackenzie there is no hint that Lewis and Clark carried with them any literature associated with Cook. But it is equally clear that Lewis must have carried the Rosa trope in his memory, probably from his days of study in Philadelphia while preparing for the expedition, having determined to save his knowledge of this literary stratagem for his own narrative.

And for this too there was precedent during Cook's second voyage, in the journal of another well-read gentleman, Wales, the astronomer aboard Cook's flagship. In response to the same sublimities that prompted the Forsters to invoke the memory of Rosa, Wales tapped into the mainstream of cultural history by summoning the poet Thomson, the other figure in Lewis's cultural dyad central to his signature moment of ineffability at the Great Falls. Wales was sufficiently familiar with Thomson's *The Seasons* that on viewing the same remarkable waterfall that affected the romantic sensibilities of all who saw it—Cook, Hodges, and the Forsters—he committed seventeen lines from Thomson's "Summer" to his journal, more or less verbatim. Wales changed a few tenses and added a stray phrase or two, for which reason, as he wrote at the end of his transcription, "I dare not write *Thomson* at the bottom: I know I have injured him; but it could not be avoided."[20]

This, however, only proves that the educated traveler like Wales was expected to be familiar with Thomson, which a great many were, for his journal was never published and thus Lewis could not have read the Thomson lines there. However, George Forster quoted from Thomson while explicating Cook's second long ice-edge foray southeast of New Zealand.

Writing on Christmas Day 1773 in the high southern latitudes of the Pacific Ocean, Forster was mesmerized by the same kind of view that had previously awed Cook. An "immense number of icy masses" drifted about the ship, which was "every moment in danger of being dashed to pieces." But here it was the "animal appetites" of the seamen, not the natural wonders themselves, that caused him to draw on Thomson's *Seasons*. Appalled at the drunken indulgences allowed by naval tradition on the Christmas holiday, Forster quoted from "Spring":

> At last, extinct each social feeling, fell
> And joyless humanity pervades
> And petrifies the heart.

It is worthy of remark that in his book Forster misspelled the poet's name, citing "Thompson," which, coincidentally or not, was the same way Lewis spelled it in his journal.[21]

Also relevant in regard to Thomson, and much closer to Lewis's zone of activity, was William Beresford's 1789 account of the maritime fur trade conducted during Captain George Dixon's voyage. One of the few books written about the Northwest Coast prior to Lewis's departure from Philadelphia, it was likely on his reading list at the APS. In a passage written in late September 1786, as Dixon's ship stood toward Nootka (notably referred to as a "long wished for port") a "most tempestuous storm of thunder and lightning came on." Indeed, the electrical storm was "so very fierce, that it blinded the people on deck for a considerable time." Beresford was one of those affected, which prompted him to reflect "how often I have thought, that nothing in nature could equal the thunder storm so beautifully described by Thomson, in his Seasons: …the majesty of the whole still heightened by the roaring of the wind, the raging of the sea, and a more than common darkness, which overspread the surrounding atmosphere."[22]

Thus, as is true of so many aspects of Enlightenment-era exploration, Lewis was not crafting his experiences, or more particularly the words describing them, de novo; instead, he was drawing on literary tradition. We may unassailably deduce which sections from Thomson's *Seasons* Lewis was recalling when he made his famous inscription about the Great Falls via the clue provided by Wales describing the great cascade in Dusky Bay. This, from "Summer:"

Thus up the mount, in airy vision rapt,
I stray, regardless whither; till the sound
Of a near fall of water every sense
Wakes from the charm of thought: swift-shrinking back,
I check my steps and view the broken scene.
    Smooth to the shelving brink a copious flood
Rolls fair and placid; where, collected all
In one impetuous torrent, down the steep
It thundering shoots, and shakes the country round.
At first, an azure sheet, it rushes broad;
Then, whitening by degrees as prone it falls,
And from the loud-resounding rocks below
Dashed in a cloud of foam, it sends aloft
A hoary mist and forms a ceaseless shower.
Nor can the tortured wave here find repose;
But, raging still amid shaggy rocks,
Now flashes o'er the scattered fragments, now
Aslant the hollow channel rapid darts;
And, falling fast from gradual slope to slope,
With wild infracted course and lessened roar,
It gains a safer bed, and steals at last
Along the mazes of the quiet vale.[23]

This poem, as indicated by several kinetic words—impetuous, thundering, foaming, and torrent, and the image of billowing mists—clearly seems to have run through Lewis's mind, even if he was, unlike Wales, unable to commit complete lines of Thomson's text to the page. Wales himself offered valuable insights as to why explorers felt compelled to embellish supposedly scientific reports with purplish passages. He wrote: "I have always thought the situation of a Traveller singularly hard. If he tells nothing that is uncommon he must be a stupid fellow to have gone so far, and brought home so little; and if he does, why…aya…He's a Traveller."[24]

Though the Great Falls of the Missouri is a grand place, in my study of the expedition I have always wondered why Lewis chose that landscape encounter for his verbal spectacular, when one considers that several ranges of the Rocky Mountains, the equally interesting rapids and falls of The Dalles of the Columbia River Gorge, or even reaching the roaring Pacific

Ocean lay ahead. Wales offers an answer to that as well, observing that "young Travellers, like young Wits, and young Girls too for that matter, are apt to let their imaginations run riot, and ever think the first that offers a Phoenix; whereas could they but have patience, another infinitely its superior would present it self—Probatum est!"[25] This last phrase, in Latin, translates to "it has been proved."

There remains one last, tantalizing prospect for literary inspiration grounded in Cook and other muses from that era, another of the best known passages in the Lewis oeuvre—his thirty-first birthday rumination of August 18, 1805. All students of the expedition are familiar with the general context of this passage. Lewis had just completed his supremely important vanguard maneuver reaching out to the Lemhi Shoshone, or more particularly, their prospective commitment of horses that would take the expedition westward into Columbia River country. Like his Great Falls composition, Lewis's reflective journal for this venture is well written in its studied, colorful phrasing and dramatic import. In many ways, Lewis seems to have perceived reaching and surmounting the Continental Divide as the capstone of his voyage, notwithstanding the fact that he stood a thousand miles from his nominal destination, Cook's Pacific. Abruptly appended at the end of a busy-day entry we read in his journal:

> This day I completed my thirty first year, and conceived that I had in all human probability now existed about half the period which I am to remain in this Sublunary world. I reflected that I had as yet done but little, very little indeed, to further the hapiness of the human race, or to advance the information of the succeeding generation. I viewed with regret the many hours I have spent in indolence, and now soarly feel the want of that information which those hours would have given me had they been judiciously expended. [B]ut since they are past and cannot be recalled, I dash from me the gloomy thought and resolved in future, to redouble my exertions and at least indeavour to promote those two primary objects of human existence, by giving them the aid of that portion of talents which nature and fortune have bestoed on me; or in future, to live for *mankind*, as I have heretofore lived *for myself.*[26]

This paragraph has long intrigued historians of the expedition who earnestly scour the journals looking for self-disclosing or self-reflective thoughts by the captains. This instance is rare, perhaps unique, and therefore remarkable. The melancholy subtext, notwithstanding the rededication to a forward outlook, can be, and has been, read as a foreshadowing of Lewis's end-of-life psychological travail. As a rejoinder, Stephen E. Ambrose noted that "it was not unusual for men of the Enlightenment to write such stuff," nodding in Jefferson's direction for an example but without further explication.[27]

Deconstructing the text, a few key words or phrases stand out which provide clues to both the identification of Lewis's hidden inspirations and the emotive profile his attempt at self-analysis provided via coded language. To start, the Latinate word "Sublunary" is very unusual. In Lewis's voluminous journal text, it appears here solely, and must be read as a kind of literary marker and psychological emblem. To take Ambrose's point, the naturalist George Forster in his account of Cook's second voyage, former Marine Corporal Ledyard in his history of Cook's third voyage, and Meares's account of his fur-trading exploits in Cook's wake all used the word. These men all did so in a common context—indigenous people were being referenced—though with varying nuances. Forster, allowing for "the imperfect state of sublunary happiness" endemic to all of humanity, found Native life in Tahiti to be as desirable as any on earth. In a related fashion, Ledyard used the term to describe the rapture of a shipmate who had fallen for a Polynesian beauty. In contrast, Meares, describing the Mowahchat of Nootka Sound, referred to their belief in the "hereafter, beyond the reach of *sublunary* sorrow."[28]

The emotional dichotomy we see in these references, roughly contemporaneous with Lewis's, betoken the extreme range of moods at the heart of human existence. This reflects one of the principal themes of English poet Edward Young's (1683–1765) influential "Night-Thoughts" (1742), especially the fugitive nature of time that serves as the subtext for Lewis's reflection, and the whipsawing humans endure between the poles of bliss and moonlight melancholy. These sentiments proved to be powerfully attractive to proto-Romantics such as Lewis. Like Thomson, Young was also on every young gentleman's reading list in the late Enlightenment.

A few short passages from Young will suffice for documentation, starting with "Night First: On Life, Death, and Immortality":

Of Time's enormous scythe, whose ample sweep
Strikes empires from the root; each moment plays
His little weapon in the narrower sphere
Of sweet domestic comfort, and cuts down
The fairest bloom of sublunary bliss.
Bliss! sublunary bliss! proud words and vain!

From "Night Second: On Time, Death, and Friendship":

O time! than gold more sacred; more a load
Than lead to fools; and fools reputed wise.
What moment granted man without account?
What years are squander'd, wisdom's debt unpaid!
Our wealth in days, all due to that discharge.
Haste, haste, he lies in wait, he's at the door,
Insidious Death, should his strong hand arrest,
No composition sets the prisoner free.[29]

The title of Young's poem perfectly reflects the nocturnal timing of Lewis's reflection, and the indictment of self-gratification and the sensual life in verse seems to echo the explorer's critique of himself in prose. Furthermore, it is interesting to note that Lewis's entry for the following day is dominated by his discussion of Shoshone gender relations—guidance to his men on what might be called sexual diplomacy in the wake of some of them having "made very polite to those tawney damsels" and an inquiry into the occurrence of venereal disease among these people.[30] In short, Lewis wrote his birthday reflection at a time of sexual temptation and was possibly fearful that he had lost his ascetic grip.

The other key word in Lewis's birthday contemplation is "indolence." This stands out because Thomson was also known for another famous allegorical poem, "The Castle of Indolence." From the Great Falls sequence we can safely assume that if Lewis read the one, he was likely familiar with the other as well. Touching on some of the same themes as Young's "Night-Thoughts," the first canto of "Indolence" can be read as an indictment of overindulgence in liquor, partying, and living a life of comfort; it speaks of a room filled with "one full-swelling bed" with its cushy pillows, "wines high-flavorourd and rich viands," and the freedom to "melt the time in love." A very telling line reads: "But not even pleasure to excess is good: What most elates then sinks the soul as low." Thomson's "Indolence" is also the likely source and inspiration behind the Rosa trope found in so many contemporary exploratory accounts, including Lewis's Great Falls of the Missouri text (discussed above). Another first canto extract begins by describing how a "pencil" can bring landscapes to life, complete with operatic atmospherics such as when "the black tempest strikes the astonished eyes." This passage ends with these five lines, trumpeting the skills of the picturesque school of art.

Now down the steep the flashing torrent flies;
The trembling sun now plays o'er the ocean blue,
And now rude mountains frown amid the skies;
Whate'er Lorrain light-touched with softening hue,
Or savage Rosa dashed, or learnéd Poussin drew.

The second canto of "The Castle of Indolence" provides the redemptive rejoinder to the boyish innocence and simplicity of "youth" that inevitably turns into the thorny reality of adulthood. In this section, diligence triumphs over idleness in the textual form of the false enchanter or wizard "Indolence" that is vanquished by the "Knight of Arts and Industry." The following lines from the poem are almost biographic as pertains to Lewis.

He knew no beverage but the flowing stream;
His tasteful well-earned food the silvan game,
Or the brown fruit with which the woodlands teem:
The same to him glad summer or the winter breme.
…he scanned the globe, those small domains,
Where restless mortals such a turmoil keep,
Its seas, its floods, its mountains, and its plains;
But more he searched the mind, and roused from sleep
Those moral seeds whence we heroic actions reap.

The foregoing passage is perfectly summed up by one other line from Thomson's poem: "Renown is not the child of indolent repose."[31] All this gets to the heart of Lewis's emotions on that night in the middle of the Rocky Mountains and the run of his conscious or unconscious thought and idealization of self.

The Lewis and Clark story has been told in many ways: as western adventure, cross-cultural encounter, military and diplomatic history, or a study of the environment. My aim here has been to show how the expedition can also be understood as a study in English literature, for every exploratory text resonates with the ambient culture that produced it. This essay is also a response to the clarion call of James P. Ronda's valedictory noted at the outset of this book. For Cook's and Lewis and Clark's stories to remain fresh and lively, scholars need to break out of the tedious sequential and directional straitjackets that bind and hinder their interpretations and risk making them irrelevant. It is only fitting that the lives of men who sought new lands and new people be studied at greater depths in new dimensions.

NOTES

1. Gary E. Moulton, ed., *The Journals of the Lewis & Clark Expedition* (Lincoln: University of Nebraska Press, 1983–2001), 4: 9.
2. Richard A. Van Orman, *The Explorers: Nineteenth-Century Expeditions in Africa and the American West* (Albuquerque: University of New Mexico Press, 1984), 140.
3. Moulton, *Journals*, 7: 10.
4. Moulton, *Journals*, 7: 11n8.
5. Ibid.
6. Ibid.
7. Ibid.
8. David L. Nicandri, *River of Promise: Lewis and Clark on the Columbia* (Bismarck, ND: Dakota Institute Press, 2009), 203–17.
9. W. Kaye Lamb, ed., *The Journals and Letters of Sir Alexander Mackenzie* (London: Cambridge University Press, 1970), 370.
10. John C. Beaglehole, ed., *The Journals of Captain James Cook on His Voyages of Discovery* (Cambridge: Cambridge University Press for the Hakluyt Society, 1955–67), 3: 1410.
11. James Cook and James King, *A Voyage to the Pacific Ocean...in the Years* [1776–80] (London: G. Nicol and T. Cadell, 1784), 2: 316.
12. Ibid., 327.
13. John Meares, *Voyages Made in the Years 1788 and 1789, from China to the North West Coast of America*, reprint ed. (New York: Da Capo Press, 1968), 263.
14. Moulton, *Journals*, 4: 284–85, 290.
15. John C. Beaglehole, ed., *The Journals of Captain James Cook on His Voyages of Discovery* (Cambridge: Cambridge University Press for the Hakluyt Society, 1961), 2: 98–99; James Cook, *A Voyage Towards the South Pole and Around the World*, Wikisource, https://en.wikisource.org/wiki/A_Voyage_Towards_the_South_pole_and_Around_the_World/Volume_I/Chapter_III. Accessed March 24, 2020.
16. Beaglehole, *Journals*, 2: 119.
17. George Forster, *A Voyage Round the World*, Nicholas Thomas and Oliver Berghof, eds. (Honolulu: University of Hawaii Press, 2000), 1: xli–xlii, 79–80.
18. Ibid., 90–91.
19. Johann Reinhold Forster, *Observations Made during a Voyage Round the World*, Nicholas Thomas, Harriet Guest, and Michael Dettelbach, eds. (Honolulu: University of Hawaii Press, 1996), 51.
20. Bernard Smith, *Imagining the Pacific in the Wake of the Cook Voyages* (New Haven, CT: Yale University Press, 1992), 141; Beaglehole, *Journals*, 2: 782–-83; 783n1.
21. George Forster, *Voyage*, 1: 290, 460n4.
22. William Beresford, *A Voyage Round the World...to the North-West Coast of America...[by] Captains Portlock and Dixon* (London: Geo. Goulding, 1789), 78, 80.
23. J. Logie Robertson, ed. *The Complete Poetical Works of James Thomson* (London: Oxford University Press, 1908), 75–76.
24. Quoted in Smith, *Imagining the Pacific*, 138.
25. Beaglehole, *Journals*, 2: 783.
26. Moulton, *Journals*, 5: 118; emphasis in the original.
27. Stephen E. Ambrose, *Undaunted Courage: Meriwether Lewis, Thomas Jefferson, and the Opening of the American West* (New York: Simon & Schuster, 1996), 280.
28. George Forster, *Voyage*, 1: 198; John Ledyard, *The Last Voyage of Captain Cook: The Collected Writings of John Ledyard*, James Zug, ed. (Washington: National Geographic, 2005), 8; Meares, *Voyages*, 270.

29. Edward Young, "The Project Gutenberg EBook of Young's 'Night Thoughts,'" https://www.gutenberg.org/files/33156/33156-h/33156-h.htm, accessed March 24, 2020, "Night-First," lines 195–99, "Night Second," lines 28–35.
30. Moulton, *Journals,* 5: 122.
31. Robertson, *Works of James Thomson*, 264–65, 274, 281–82, 295.

THE MISSING JOURNALS:

SOME CLUES ON THE UPPER MISSOURI

In his introduction to the journals of the Lewis and Clark Expedition, Gary E. Moulton addressed the question of whether the full documentary record associated with the voyage had been passed down to posterity. Moulton stipulated that at Fort Mandan Meriwether Lewis said seven men were keeping journals in addition to himself and William Clark. Since Lewis directed all the sergeants to keep field notes, Moulton deduced "we should assume that Sergeant Nathaniel Pryor...kept a journal, but one has never been found, if it ever existed."[1] If we also assume that the journal kept by Sergeant Charles Floyd, who died the summer before the expedition reached Fort Mandan, was *not* to be counted among that number, then we know three of the seven: Pryor, plus Sergeants John Ordway and Patrick Gass, the latter elevated to that status after the death of Floyd. Who then, were the other four?

One can be immediately identified—Private Joseph Whitehouse, whose original field notes and fair copy were annotated by Moulton in his comprehensive version of the expedition's extant journals. In addition to the mysterious disappearance of Pryor's record, Moulton was confident that journal keeper number five was Private Robert Frazer, sensibly citing the fact that he was given permission to publish his notes by Lewis. Frazer issued a prospectus in 1806 but in Moulton's words "the publication never took place and the journal is apparently lost."[2] It may be uncharitable to say so, but if Frazer's journal emulated the apparent competence of his chart making, we haven't missed much. Lewis probably inspected Frazer's (and the other journals) from time to time, if only to aid his own memory of events. The fact that Lewis strenuously objected to publication of Gass's account after agreeing to Frazer's request could be read as a contemporary admission that the latter was not going to provide much in the way of expeditionary insight or literary competition.

Thus, as Moulton phrased it, we are left with the need "to locate two other journalists," again *if* that of the deceased Floyd was not one of the seven Lewis had in mind in his Mandan enumeration. In Lewis and Clark lore it has long been thought that George Shannon was a journalkeeper, principally on the basis that he helped Nicholas Biddle prepare the published account that emerged in 1814. However, Moulton states Biddle "never referred to a diary by Shannon." Moulton also asserted "there is some evidence that Private Alexander Willard kept a journal and that it was accidentally destroyed." And that is where he left the matter: "Lewis's seven journalists…[were] Gass, Ordway, Frazer, Pryor, Whitehouse, and perhaps Floyd and Willard."[3]

I believe there is evidence internal to the journals of Lewis and Clark that is highly suggestive as to the identity of the two missing journal keepers (not counting Floyd, who becomes in effect the eighth journalist), and they are *not* Shannon or Willard. In coming to this determination I have been heavily influenced by my reading of the equally voluminous journals of Captain James Cook. As noted in the previous chapter and elsewhere in this book, exploratory journals, certainly in their published form and often only as a manuscript, are more properly thought of as polished literary productions, not unrefined diaries. Both forms intend to convey a faithful recapitulation of events but they have different narrative objectives; in fact, largely as a result of the immense popularity of travel literature, which itself owed much to accounts of Cook's voyages, explorers' journals were framed with certain literary conventions in mind.

The storytelling custom at issue in the present instance is place naming. Let's take Cook as an example. Over the course of three epic voyages, principally in the Pacific Basin but covering the South Atlantic and Indian Ocean as well, Cook had an almost limitless opportunity to name places he saw, and in some cases he was the first person of European origin to visit or discover them. Drawing on his country's naval tradition, Cook would occasionally name islands, mountains, or coastal headlands after biographical figures. This included, in two extraordinary situations where his ships were rescued by a near-miraculous turn of events, a nod in the direction of Providence. At other times a name would be inspired by an atmospheric condition, a topographic resemblance to a landscape in the British Isles, or one of Great Britain's subjurisdictions (most famously New South Wales in Australia). If Cook was truly at a loss for inspiration he would scan the Church of England's Book of Common Prayer and name a place after that day's saint. This orientation to the liturgical calendar was increasingly common on his third voyage, by which time Cook was running out of admirals, nobles, parliamentarians, or even experiences to name places after.

But there was one sure clue indicating a place of unusual importance to Cook—when he named a feature after his sovereign, George III (or one of his progeny), or his patron John Montagu, Lord Sandwich, the first lord of the Admiralty. On his second voyage, commissioned to find *Terra Australis Incognita* during which he circumnavigated Antarctica (a continent for which he secured mankind's first intimation thereof), Cook made two mission-centric discoveries of the highest order and named them accordingly. Having spent two long years vacating the Indian and Pacific Oceans of prospects for the southern continent, in the austral summer of 1775 Cook first found and then named the *"Isle of Georgia* in honor of H. Majesty," east of Cape Horn. The usually laconic Cook did not elaborate on names, no more than Lewis did. Thus, we learn from the voyage's assistant naturalist George Forster that since "the main object of our voyage [was] to explore the high southern latitude[s],…it would be proper to name this land after the monarch who had set on foot our expedition." This mountainous and heavily glaciated island, only twenty miles wide but one hundred sixteen miles long, was later renamed South Georgia and made famous in exploration history by Ernest Shackleton's heroic voyage to its shore from Elephant Island. Cook suspected, incorrectly he soon learned, that this island might be his only geographic find in the targeted zone of discovery set for him by the Admiralty, so when he reached its southeastern extremity and realized this new land's insular character—as opposed to its promise as the headland for an entire continent—he named it Cape Disappointment, the most emotive place name in the entire Cook oeuvre.[4]

However, later that same month of January 1775, while heading to Cape Town and thus concluding the voyage's discovery phase, Cook was determined to track down an elusive headland and/or island reportedly discovered by the French explorer Jean-Baptiste Charles Bouvet de Lozier. Sailing slightly south of east from South Georgia toward the Indian Ocean, Cook encountered several previously undiscovered islands, the most southern of which, at the remarkably specific "observed latitude" of 59°13'30" S on the meridian equidistant from South America and Africa, he called "*Southern Thule* because it is the most southern land that have yet been descovered." While tacking about these several icy lands in order to conduct his reconnaissance, Cook named a passage between two of them Forsters Bay (for the expedition's chief naturalist), after which the great navigator reported "we got sight of a new coast." Cook named this location Cape Montagu after the family name of the Admiralty's first lord. The nomenclature of a "bay" and "cape" is indicative of the fact that in the thick fog Cook concluded, mistakenly, "that the whole was connected," that is, it formed a single mountainous icebound coast. With his crew fatigued and ship well-worn, Cook did not think it prudent to venture closer, but after spotting still more islets on his northward track toward Cape Town, Cook, after reflecting upon the week's serial discoveries, "concluded that what we had seen, which I named *Sandwich Land* was either a group of Islands or else a point of the Continent, for I firmly beleive that there is a tract of land near the Pole." Which is to say, Cook determined to name one of the voyage's most noteworthy discoveries, perhaps one of continental proportions, after his principal Admiralty patron.[5]

For the aforementioned exigent reasons, Cook was forced to leave the matter there. On the master map showing the track of Cook's three voyages across the surface of the globe produced after his death, "Sandwich Land" was tantalizingly inscribed. But the Sandwich story does not end there, because on his ensuing voyage in search of the Northwest Passage, Cook again literally stumbled upon another island chain, except it was located in the "light airs and calms" of the tropics and inhabited. These we know as the Hawaiian Islands, arguably the greatest of Cook's discoveries. This assertion is not limited to geographic import. Noting that the natives were "of the same Nation as the people of Otahiete and the other islands we had lately visited," Cook completed his discernment of the great Polynesian dispersion that spread across the Pacific and runs from New Zealand in the west, Easter Island in the east, and Hawaii to the north. The so-called Polynesian Triangle is one of Enlightenment-era ethnology's greatest breakthroughs. But the more important point for present consideration is that in recognizing the significance of his discovery, one that is self-evident from posterity's vantage, Cook named these the "*Sandwich Islands*, in honour of the Earl of Sandwich," the Admiralty's first lord. Later in the same voyage, when Cook was the first to authoritatively chart the separation of Asia from North America at the Bering Strait, he named it "*Cape Prince of Wales*" after the reigning monarch's heir apparent and future King George

IV. He did so because the Alaskan headland "is the more remarkable by being the Western extremity of all America hitherto known."[6]

With this quick survey we see how Cook modeled the behavior of naming the most important places he discovered after his patrons and other luminaries. We also know from what Clay Jenkinson calls Lewis's "single greatest" journal entry[7] that the American explorer consciously fashioned his venture after Cook when the expedition left Fort Mandan looking for the headwaters of the Missouri. If we deconstruct Lewis's place naming we can see how he followed the same convention as did the British naval captain. As a collateral effort, we can use this pattern to discern the identities of the missing journal keepers.

It has long been an axiom in Lewis and Clark scholarship that, to use the helpful expression that Jenkinson has popularized, "the discovery phase of the expedition" began with the first leg upstream from Fort Mandan.[8] As John Logan Allen points out, "on their trip from the Missouri's mouth to the Mandan villages, Lewis and Clark were traversing a portion of the trans-Missouri West which was both known in a real sense and understood by them to be a region for which the available geographical information was reliable."[9] Allen is referring to the fur traders who, over the course of several generations, routinely made the voyage Lewis and Clark conducted in 1804, as did explorers John Evans and James Mackay, who mapped that stretch of the river only a few years before. For this reason, the American captains had few opportunities to name places during their first year in the field. Their most noteworthy additions were "4th of July 1804 Creek" near Atchison, Kansas, and "Floyds river," thus honoring the sergeant's burial spot nearby on "the top of a high round hill over looking the [Missouri] river."[10]

Parlaying the title of Joseph Conrad's novel, Stephen E. Ambrose melodramatically called Lewis's departure from Fort Mandan as a voyage into "a heart of darkness." He also went on to suggest that Lewis "could not imagine" the west's landscapes and rivers "because no American had ever seen them." Strictly speaking, this latter assertion is true, and equally so his contention that Lewis knew "from now on, until he reached the Pacific and returned, he would be making history."[11] The textual seed for Ambrose's historiographic confidence lies in the rhetorical power of Lewis's April 7, 1805, journal entry in which he likened his "little fleet" to "those of Columbus or Capt. Cook." The operative line, however, is this one: "we were now about to penetrate a country at least two thousand miles in width, *on which the foot of civillized man had never trodden.*"[12] Expanding on Lewis's original text, Jenkinson writes: "Everything up to this moment had been a shakedown cruise, a journey to the far edge of the known world, but still within the precinct of the known world. Now finally Lewis could regard himself legitimately as an authentic explorer."[13]

This scholarly consensus is not wrong, but it is overextended. In a helpful paragraph in his seminal study of the expedition, Allen made a distinction between "real knowledge"—information gleaned empirically by commercial or military enterprises in the field and the associated "accounts of travelers and observers"—and a "second and more important kind of knowledge" that he termed "'perceived knowledge,' or lore which is evaluated on the basis of accuracy as it is understood by the explorers themselves."[14] Aided by Allen's second category, it can be safely asserted that upon leaving Fort Mandan Lewis and Clark were *not* jumping off into the unknown. They had avidly inquired of their wintertime Mandan and Hidatsa neighbors about the direction and nature of the river farther upstream. This is a textbook example of "perceived knowledge," and, as every student of the expedition knows, the captains acted upon it routinely. Lewis and Clark's native informants provided a virtual checklist of features for which they were to be on the lookout as they headed west. As I noted elsewhere, "Lewis, in his comprehensive summary of geographic findings…written at Fort Mandan, concluded with a forecast of the Missouri River's tributaries expected to be encountered during the forthcoming season of discovery." This catalogue proves he was not heading into a heart of darkness. Indeed, it would have been foolhardy if Lewis hadn't gathered information "from a number of individuals questioned separately and at different times. [T]he information thus obtained has been carefully compared, and those points only, in which they generally agreed, have been retained."[15] Mandan and Hidatsa maps might not have been as graphic as those of Evans and Mackay but they were just as useful.

All of this is apparent in Lewis and Clark's pattern of place naming from Fort Mandan to the Great Falls of the Missouri. A quick scan of their atlas and journals shows their mirroring of Native understandings in the naming, or rather recognition, of such key progress points as the Yellowstone, White Earth, Milk, and Medicine Rivers. Otherwise, their charts of streams and related text are peppered with prosaic names drawn from locally distinctive animal species (for example, geese, porcupines, blowflies, grouse, turtles, magpies) or topographic conditions (dry creek and river beds, or burnt-over country). They also named a few creeks and other places after expedition members (Privates George Gibson, William Bratton, Peter Weiser, Silas Goodrich, and Richard Windsor) for nondescript reasons between May 13 and May 25, 1805, in the expansive plains country of eastern Montana.

More noteworthy was the earlier naming of "Sharbono's Creek" just a week out from Mandan. Its christening was prompted when, as Lewis noted, "our interpreter" had previously "encamped several weeks on it with a hunting party of Indians." Later that spring, the name of his spouse, Sacagawea, was inscribed upon a river that was a tributary to the Musselshell just above its own confluence with the Missouri. The timing of this name placement was not a coincidence either. On May 14 in the very middle of the modern state of Montana, a squall of wind struck one of the pirogues broadside and nearly sank her. More alarmingly, this particular craft carried what Lewis described as "our papers, Instruments, books medicine, a great part of our merchandize and in short almost every article indispensibly necessary to…the success of the enterprize." Characteristically, however, it was Clark who noted in his description of the event that "the articles which floated out was nearly all caught by the Squar who was in the rear." It almost seems that this accident, which Clark added "had like to have cost us deerly," prompted Lewis to recognize that there was an Indian woman participating in the expedition because he mentioned Sacagawea by name for the first time. Probably drawing on the help of Toussaint Charbonneau or Clark, he spelled her name phonetically in his journal, a version he applied later when he named a stream after her. Recognition for meritorious service was in keeping with the conventions of travel literature, but her place naming is also part of another pattern evident in the denomination of streams in Montana—the recognition of girlfriends or female acquaintances (particularly the names Martha, Judith, and Maria), a typology that Prince Maximillian, the mid-nineteenth explorer and patron of Karl Bodmer, scorned for its frivolity.[16]

If there was a point in the voyage where Lewis and Clark truly stepped over the edge of the known world it was above the Great Falls. From the Indians at Fort Mandan the captains hazily understood that the Missouri was formed by three tributaries in or near the mountains, but above the falls the land was truly *Terra Borealis Incognita*. Lewis virtually said as much on the no less auspicious date of July 4, 1805. In an underappreciated few lines of text, written in anticipation of leaving the friendly confines of the falls district they had known about for almost a year, Lewis explained the rationale for not dividing the party by sending some men back downstream to St. Louis. He feared that doing so would hurt the morale of "those who would in such case remain, and might possibly hazzard the fate of the expedition." This was because "we all beleive that we are now about to enter on the most perilous and difficult part of our voyage." In other words, the real work of the expedition was about to begin.[17]

The Lewis and Clark Expedition thus entered the true zone of discovery on July 15, when they proceeded upstream beyond Clark's canoe-making camp, the latter made necessary by Lewis's iron boat fiasco at the upper portage camp. Echoing the adrenaline-infused euphoria that permeated his journal the previous April leaving Fort Mandan, Lewis wrote: "At 10 A. M. we once more saw ourselves fairly under way much to my joy and I beleive that of every individual who compose the party." Clear textual evidence that something was now tangibly different is reflected in the fact that Lewis established a new and noteworthy pattern for naming places that day, rivers in particular, since they were the most relevant topographic feature encountered. Traveling the very first upriver segment south of the falls neighborhood that had been their home for weeks, Lewis named a stream flowing into the Missouri from the southeast near modern Ulm, Montana, "in honour of Mr. Robert Smith the Secretary of the Navy," a usage that endures.[18] In isolation this is an odd designation, being applied nearly in the center of the continent and therefore as far away as is possible to conceive from U.S. naval operations. But the key word is not the secretary's title—"honour" is. As we saw with Captain Cook, when explorers start consciously *honoring* people by ascribing the names of dignitaries to some remote part of the world, the traveler is saying something about himself as much as the honoree: something important has been discovered or is happening.

Choosing to name a river after an otherwise obscure figure like Smith only makes sense in light of immediately ensuing events. The next day, Lewis's topographic sensibility told him he had reached the spot "where the river enters the Rocky Mountains." On July 18 he named the waterway that debouches into the canyon "Dearborn's river," after Secretary of War Henry Dearborn. On the surface this name makes more sense since Lewis was a member of that chain of command; in a manner of speaking Dearborn was his boss. More to the point, by naming the river in this way Lewis applied a military-service toponym paralleling Smith River.[19]

It's at this stage in the voyage that the naming business gets truly interesting because that same day Lewis denominated "Ordway's creek," a
name which regrettably did not endure.[20] Sgt. Ordway was, after only the
captains themselves, the most accomplished journal keeper, certainly in
terms of regularity. Ordway's contribution to the expedition is here otherwise unremarked upon by Lewis, but his having been honored in the same
fashion as two of President Thomas Jefferson's junior cabinet members is,
as the captains liked to say, worthy of remark. To wit: this place name is an
early indicator in the expedition's record as to who among the detachment
was keeping a journal, as explained below.

Beginning on July 19, Lewis guided the canoes upstream against a
strong current using principally the "toe rope" but also "the pole as the
river is not now so deep," while Clark commanded a small overland vanguard. After passing above the *"gates of the rocky mountains,"* Clark came
upon a "butifull *Creek*...which meanders thro' a butifull Vallie of great
extent, I call after Sgt Pryor." Because the captains were separated, this
incident suggests, if it doesn't actually prove, that between themselves they
had at some point conformed a naming strategy. Indeed, when Lewis also
emerged from the canyon he attempted to name yet another stream after
Pryor before learning Clark had already appended the sergeant's name to a
different creek. Assenting to Clark's previous application of Pryor's name,
Lewis renamed the stream he was originally intending to honor after his
colleague as "white Earth Creek...from the circumstance of the natives
procuring a white paint on this Crek, [*sic*]" now known as Beaver Creek
in Broadwater County, Montana. (This intelligence was either gleaned at
Fort Mandan, or more likely, in reflection of the retrospective nature of
Lewis's relatively polished journal for this leg of the journey, was knowledge that came to him after meeting the Shoshone Indians.) Be that as
it may, for our purposes the more important point is that in the process
of reconciling his own record of events with Clark's earlier denomination
of Pryor Creek, Lewis penned adulatory text which intervening circumstances dictated that he write over, referring to him as "a steady valuable
and usefull member of our party."[21] In this somewhat confused fashion, the
two most senior sergeants were honored in succession.

Once both captains had separately entered the country south of the
canyon where "the valley became wider," Lewis named the next affluent
"Pott's Creek after John Potts one of our party." In retrospect it seems

surprising that, after memorializing two cabinet members followed by the senior enlisted men, Lewis should choose to honor John Potts, otherwise one of the most obscure members of the expedition. Perhaps for that reason his name on the landscape did not endure. The mystery may be left there, except that on July 23 Lewis named "Whitehous's Creek, after Josph. Whitehouse one of the party." This (understated) mention utilizes the same laconic usage applied to Potts, except it is commonly known that Whitehouse was a journal keeper whose field notes came down to posterity. Then, on the final approach to the three forks Lewis named "Gass's Creek…after Sergt. Patric Gass one of our party." Gass was the junior sergeant, elevated by election of the men after Floyd's death, but a more than usually important member of the expedition because he also kept a journal that actually made it to print before the authorized edition did.[22]

Our literary story begins its crescendo on July 25, when Clark reached the forks of the Missouri, a topographic feature that he did not elaborate upon, probably in deference to his co-commander. Lewis was still two days travel behind him farther downstream but during this transit he named "Howard's Creek after Thomas P. Howard one of our party," using the now formulaic description and thereby bracketing known journal keeper Whitehouse with the preceding naming of "Pott's Creek." On July 27 Lewis, and the trailing detachment poling or hauling the water craft upstream, finally coursed through a brace of limestone cliffs, whereupon "the country opens suddonly to extensive and beatifull plains and meadows which appear to be surrounded in every direction with distant and lofty mountains; supposing this to be the three forks of the Missouri I halted the party." Lewis deemed this place "an essential point in the geography of this western part of the Continent" because it served as the jumping-off point for the assault on the connecting link, creating an imagined Northwest Passage that was central to the expedition's mission. In service of that vision, the southwestern fork drew his attention because "it's direction is much more promising than any other." On his corresponding record of courses and distances traveled, Lewis named the southeast fork "in honor of Albert Gallatin Secretary of the Treasury…the Middle fork…in honor of James Maddison the Secretary of State." Lewis called the southwest fork, the one seemingly aimed at the presumed headwaters of the Columbia River, after "that illustrious per[s]onage Thomas Jefferson President of the United States."[23]

Reflecting upon this matter in his journal proper on July 28, Lewis recorded that he named several streams "after the President of the United States and the Secretaries of the Treasury and state having previously named one river in honour of the Secretaries of War and Navy."[24] With this text Lewis explicitly brackets a pivotal, mission-centric segment of the trail with the greatest luminaries in the Jefferson administration, including the president himself, while similarly enclosing other streams named after the three sergeants (Ordway, Pryor, Gass) and three privates (Potts, Whitehouse, Howard). As noted earlier, the sergeants were ordered to maintain journals, two of which have come down to our age. As for the privates, they had been joined to very distinguished company. Among them was one of the best journal keepers of all, Whitehouse. All this suggests that the authors of two of the missing journals are Potts and Howard, in addition to Pryor.

Some may say that the pattern of names is coincidental but a subsequent turn of events indicates otherwise. Recall that it was during this stage of the expedition that Clark became afflicted by sore feet by virtue of "walking over the flint, & constantly Stuck full [of] Prickley Pear thorns" while in the van. Learning of this shortly thereafter Lewis somewhat smugly crowed to himself that he had "guarded or reather fortified my feet against them by soaling my mockersons with the hide of the buffaloe." Though it had been previously determined for Clark to be on the point in search of the Shoshone Indians, and more particularly their horses, Lewis inherited this assignment out of necessity, no doubt to his secret glee. When Lewis jumped off from the Missouri's forks for the Columbia River and exploratory glory, the very first name he appended to an affluent of the exalted Jefferson River was after "Robert Frazier one of our party," a stream now called Boulder Creek near Cardwell, Montana.[25]

It is worth recalling here that Frazer had been court-martialed in March 1804 during the expedition's shakedown phase, along with John Shields the armorer and the ineffable John Colter. We know from Clark that Shields and Colter "asked the forgiveness & & promised to doe better in future," but there's no mention of Frazer trying to ingratiate himself back into good standing. Indeed, Frazer was going to be a part of the detachment sent back to St. Louis from Fort Mandan but managed to sufficiently redeem himself (perhaps by volunteering to keep a journal?) so as to be added to the party heading farther west. He was assigned to Gass's mess, replacing the even more troublesome Moses Reed. In any event, on the run-up to the expedition's pivotal moment we find Lewis naming a tributary to the prized Jefferson River after Frazer, just downstream from two more significant branches of the Jefferson that Lewis named the Philanthropy and Wisdom forks "in commemoration of two of those cardinal virtues, which have so eminently marked that deservedly selibrated character through life."[26]

In sum, the journals of the Lewis and Clark Expedition, informed as they were by the conventions of travel literature, carry within them the internal evidence that identifies the seven journal keepers (in addition to the captains) enumerated at Fort Mandan. A working typology follows: (1) those whose work is extant (Ordway, Gass, Whitehouse); (2) those whose record was once known to exist or from circumstantial evidence likely existed (Frazer, Pryor); and (3) the truly missing journals (Potts, Howard).

It would be fair to ask whether there is any other circumstantial evidence that warrants listing Potts and Howard on this speculative roster of journal keepers. Both of these men were assigned to the expedition from Captain John Campbell's infantry regiment stationed at South West Point, Tennessee (at present day Kingston), on November 24, 1803. Though not as distinguished in Lewis and Clark lore as the legendary "Nine Young Men from Kentucky" (which included Floyd, Colter, the Field brothers, and five others who joined the captains as they proceeded down the Ohio), this eight-man unit was led into Camp Dubois on December 22 by the army's civilian guide/hunter George Drouillard, who had already joined the expedition. In the orthodox understanding of the Lewis and Clark story, this group's leading figure was Corporal Richard Warfington, a man originally intended for the permanent western party but eventually given the assignment to conduct the return outfit and the first set of reports back to St. Louis from Fort Mandan aboard the expedition's keelboat in the spring of 1805. When Campbell's detachment (also including permanent member Hugh Hall) first arrived at Camp Dubois, their "readiness" was questioned by Clark, the commandant there. In the event, four of the eight washed out, leading Moulton to suggest "that Campbell had sent some of his less desirable men."[27]

And, as a matter of fact, Hall and Howard were court-martialed at disparate points on the trail west. But then, a dozen different men got into disciplinary trouble at some point including, at Camp Dubois, probable journal keeper Frazer and known writer Whitehouse (in addition to an expedition member who later deserted the army). Given the self-evident circumstances that proved Warfington's trustworthiness to secure a detached command, and Whitehouse's and Frazer's, which rescued their reputations with the captains (helping them to obtain a spot in the party after its shakedown phase), one should not read too much into the fact that Howard and Potts came to the expedition from a larger set that was less than stellar as a whole. Indeed, as noted earlier in regard to Frazer, it is conceivable that keeping a journal was either a demand from the commanders or a means for these enlisted men to ingratiate themselves back into their superiors' good graces.

Howard was reared in Massachusetts, enhancing the likelihood of his securing an early education in literacy and numeracy. In the early republic, the New England states had the highest literacy rates; in the towns and cities of Massachusetts the ratio approached 100 percent.[28] Howard joined the army in his early twenties in 1801 and dutifully served until 1808. Potts was an immigrant from Germany, though we don't know at what age, and was a miller before joining the army in 1800. We must assume he spoke English, and his being a tradesman suggests he possessed a common set of social and business skills. Like all of northwestern Europe by the end of the Enlightenment, literacy was essential to commercial, community, and cultural life across all socioeconomic classes. Correspondingly, the rates were high in the Germanic provinces. Although there is ultimately no way of proving how well educated Potts was, he was an adequately reliable figure to secure a place in Manuel Lisa's fur trade company. He died in 1807 at the Three Forks in the same fracas Colter barely survived. Colter, Moulton once averred, is "probably the only member of the Corps whose fame does not rest primarily on his service with the expedition,"[29] and Potts's association with him, if only in death, is distinguished company. So too is his placement in the register of important place names on the upper Missouri, an inclusion that satisfied Lewis and Clark's efforts to memorialize figures central to the expedition's story.

——————— N O T E S ———————

1. Gary E. Moulton, ed., *The Journals of the Lewis & Clark Expedition* (Lincoln: University of Nebraska Press, 1983–2001), 2: 544.

2. Moulton, *Journals*, 1: map 124; 2: 517.

3. Moulton, *Journals*, 2: 544–45.

4. John C. Beaglehole, ed., *The Journals of Captain James Cook on His Voyages of Discovery* (Cambridge: Cambridge University Press for the Hakluyt Society, 1955–67), 2: 625.

5. Beaglehole, *Journals*, 2: 632–33, 636–37.

6. Beaglehole, *Journals,* 3: 263–64, 278, 409.

7. Clay Jenkinson, *The Character of Meriwether Lewis: Explorer in the Wilderness* (Bismarck, ND: Dakota Institute Press, 2011), 16.

8. Ibid., 16.

9. John Logan Allen, *Lewis and Clark and the Image of the American Northwest* (New York: Dover, 1991), 254.

10. Moulton, *Journals,* 2: 347, 495.

11. Stephen E. Ambrose, *Undaunted Courage: Meriwether Lewis, Thomas Jefferson, and the Opening of the American West* (New York: Simon & Schuster, 1996), 216.

12. Moulton, *Journals,* 4: 9, emphasis added.

13. Jenkinson, *Character,* 16.

14. Allen, *Lewis and Clark,* 253.

15. David L. Nicandri, *River of Promise: Lewis and Clark on the Columbia* (Bismarck, ND: Dakota Institute Press, 2009), 17.

16. Moulton, *Journals,* 4: 36, 152, 154, 171.

17. Moulton, *Journals,* 4: 359, 361.

18. Moulton, *Journals,* 4: 382.

19. Moulton, *Journals,* 4: 386, 398.

20. Moulton, *Journals,* 4: 398.

21. Moulton, *Journals,* 4: 403, 405, 411–12, 417.

22. Moulton, *Journals,* 4: 406–7, 420, 426.

23. Moulton, *Journals,* 4: 430, 434–35, 437.

24. Moulton, *Journals,* 5: 7.

25. Moulton, *Journals,* 4: 404–5; 5: 28.

26. Moulton, *Journals,* 2: 183; 3: 153; 5:54.

27. Moulton, *Journals,* 2: 139.

28. Jack Lynch, "'Every Man Able to Read': Literacy in Early America," Colonial Williamsburg, www.history.org/foundation/journal/winter11/literacy.cfm, accessed November 1, 2018.

29. Moulton, *Journals,* 2: 515.

CHAPTER 5

THE ILLUSION OF
CAPE DISAPPOINTMENT

On October 31, 1805, William Clark stood on a promontory on the north bank of the Columbia River, overlooking the tail end of a narrow, four-mile-long stretch of rapids. The Great Chute, as Clark called it, was the last major obstacle faced by the Corps of Volunteers for Northwestern Discovery in its quest to reach the Pacific Ocean. Beyond the rapids, Clark later noted in his journal, the river "widened and had everry appearance of being effected by the tide."[1]

We can imagine the anticipation that Clark, Meriwether Lewis, and the rest of the party felt while in camp that night and in the days following their descent down the Great Chute. The expedition still had many miles to go before reaching the Pacific, but their dugout canoes were now riding waters of the lower Columbia ruled by both current and intermittently helpful tides. Lewis had left the Atlantic seaboard more than two years before, and it had been six months since the explorers had departed the Mandan villages, located in present-day North Dakota. Memories of their laborious ascent of the Missouri, the arduous crossing of the Bitterroot Mountains, and the water-crested dash down the Columbia receded day by day with the gathering realization that the long-awaited Pacific was nearly at hand.

For the preceding quarter century, European and American maritime explorers had sailed in and around the same grand confluence formed where the Columbia meets the Pacific. In 1775, Spain's Bruno de Hezeta perceived the hint of a large river and inscribed this sketchy prospect on his nation's charts of the North Pacific. John Meares, pursuing maritime fur trade opportunities on behalf of British commercial interests that were first popularized in published accounts that detailed James Cook's third and final voyage, flirted with fame in 1788 when he coasted the same shores Cook had outlined in 1778 but did not explore because his mission was centered on higher latitudes. But unlike Hezeta, Meares concluded that the headland sighted at the forty-sixth parallel merely guarded a bay off the ocean, instead of forming the gateway into the heart of the continent that it proved to be. He accordingly named it Cape Disappointment.[2]

The American fur trader Robert Gray finally crossed the bar of the river that would bear the name of his ship, *Columbia Rediviva*, in May 1792. Five months later, Captain George Vancouver of the British navy arrived at the Columbia's mouth and sent a subordinate, Lieutenant William Broughton, to explore the river. Broughton traveled more than a hundred miles upstream, to the vicinity of present-day Portland. Vancouver related the details of Broughton's journey in the account of his Pacific explorations published in 1798. This three-volume work, which contained a detailed map of the Columbia estuary, was avidly read by contemporary geographers. Alexander Mackenzie, who had reached Pacific tidewater in 1793 but had not yet written his account, concluded that the great river he took south from present-

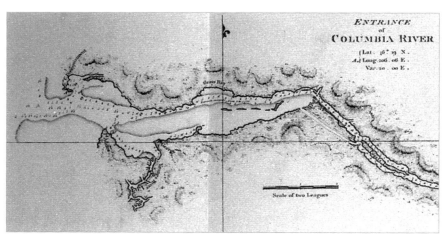

George Vancouver, *Entrance of Columbia River*, inset from *A Chart Showing Part of the Coast of N. W. North America* (1798). Vancouver's chart of the Columbia estuary was Lewis and Clark's primary source about the lower river. One principal detail in Vancouver's image varied from reality: the headland opposite and to the north of Tongue Point on the south bank of the river is far more prominent than depicted here. (Compare to cartographer Martin Plamondon II's more accurate depiction on page 78). Courtesy of the Washington State Historical Society. WSHS 1911.5.4.

Ocian in View! O! The joy, by Roger Cooke (2003). Courtesy of the Washington State Historical Society. WSHS 2005.22.79.

day north-central British Columbia (before cutting over to the coast) was the same river Gray had discovered and Broughton charted. Mackenzie was wrong (the river he had actually been on was later discerned as the Fraser) but by conjoining his river work with Vancouver's failure to find the second generation of the Northwest Passage he created the successor version of that cartographic image: a network of interconnected rivers. Vancouver's account and charts were also Thomas Jefferson's primary sources about the lower Columbia when he dispatched the Lewis and Clark Expedition in furtherance of the vision Mackenzie outlined in 1801 in *Voyages from Montreal*.[3]

On November 7, 1805, a week after Clark first noticed tidal action on the lower river, the expedition reached the vicinity of Pillar Rock, a prominent landmark lying just offshore on the north side of the estuary. Clark was now certain he could see the Pacific. Lewis is usually cited as the great voice of the expedition, but one presumed shout by his co-leader has come down through history as the most famous declaration in the record of their joint command: "*Ocian in view!* O! the joy."[4]

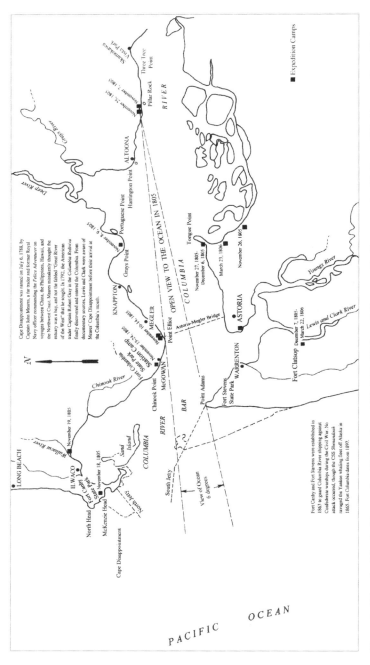

Ocean in View, by Martin Plamondon II, *Lewis and Clark Trail Maps: A Cartographic Reconstruction* (Pullman: Washington State University Press, 2004), 3: 62. Plamondon's projection shows how William Clark mistook Point Ellice (where the Astoria-Megler Bridge lands on the river's north bank) for Cape Disappointment. Courtesy of Washington State University Press.

For over one hundred years, however, historians have been dousing Clark's observation with water as cold as the Columbia's, claiming that what he actually saw was not the true Pacific but merely the river's lower estuary.[5] This notion has prevailed since 1905, when Reuben Gold Thwaites observed that Point Adams, projecting from the Oregon side of the inlet, would have blocked a direct line of sight between Pillar Rock and the ocean. Thwaites evidently did not realize that Point Adams, which in the late nineteenth century had been artificially extended to aid navigation, was much smaller in 1805 and would not have obstructed Clark's view toward the ocean. Rex Ziak presents this revisionist concept in *In Full View*, his book about Lewis and Clark on the lower Columbia, as does Martin Plamondon II in his three-volume reconstruction of Lewis and Clark's trail maps.[6] But neither author goes far enough in his analysis.

The sequence of events leading up to Clark's famed but oft-disputed exclamation had commenced two days earlier, on November 5. That night, the captains posted a guard over the canoes to protect them from the vagaries of tides rising and falling by as much as three feet. After getting underway the following morning, the party passed a notable "Knob of high land," later called Coffin Rock, so named because it was the site of Indian burials.[7] Proceeding on a generally westerly course (the Columbia makes its last major turn near its confluence with the Cowlitz River, entering from the north), the corps passed a "Clift of verry high land" and camped on a narrow "bold rockey Shore." This terrain is traversed today by Washington Route 4 from Stella to the vicinity of Cathlamet, the approximate location of camp that evening.[8]

The explorers now found Indians who could speak "a fiew words of english." The Natives indicated they had recently traded with a certain "Mr. Haley," presumably a merchant sea captain, giving rise to the possibility that he or some other American or British trader might still be present on the coast.[9]

When the party set out at 8 a.m. on the seventh, the fog was thick, necessitating the services of an Indian pilot who, wearing "Salors" garb, guided the explorers through a network of islands and sloughs. One canoe became separated from the rest for most of the day but reunited with the party that evening. As part of the daily course and distance records Clark kept in his elkskin-bound field notes, he recorded: "we are in view of the opening of the Ocian, which Creates great joy."[10]

This was the first—and, it is important to note, the most understated—version of three declarations made by Clark about sighting the ocean. He does not dwell on the occasion but in the very next sentence turns his attention to Pillar Rock, describing this columnar specimen of basalt as a "remarkable rock of about 50 feet high and about 20 feet Diameter…opposit our Camp about 1/2 a mile from Shore." Of the other journalists, only Joseph Whitehouse mentioned the rock's characteristic form, noting that it "had very much the resemlance of a Tower." Surprisingly, neither Whitehouse nor either of the two other enlisted journal keepers—John Ordway and Patrick Gass—noted any particular excitement in camp that night.[11]

When Clark wrote his reflection for the day in his regular journal, he expanded the entry found in his original elkskin field notes. This more frequently cited passage reads: "Great joy in camp we are in *View* of the *Ocian*, this great Pacific Octean which we [have] been So long anxious to See. and the roreing or noise made by the waves brakeing on the rockey Shores (as I Suppose) may be heard distictly."[12]

Clark's final version of this sighting—the shortest of the three, found in his recapitulation of courses and distances for the trip down the Columbia—is one of the most famous exclamations in the history of exploration: "*Ocian in view*! O! the joy." Clark almost certainly wrote these last two passages months after the fact.[13]

Gary E. Moulton and most other scholars, including the influential John Logan Allen, have followed Thwaites's 1905 assertion that from Pillar Rock the explorers were looking out at the Columbia estuary, not the ocean per se. Clark, in other words, had gotten ahead of himself.[14] Lewis's observations aren't known, since he either wasn't writing in his journal at the time or his journal for this period has been lost. Stephen E. Ambrose muses that Lewis might have written about this "moment of triumph" with the same flair found in his descriptions of the White Cliffs, Great Falls, and Three Forks of the Missouri—passages that "set the standard" for exploratory text. Echoing the conventional view, Ambrose says that Clark was "a bit premature" in his exclamation that the Pacific now lay before them.[15]

But caution should be taken before concluding that Clark was mistaken—especially (as Ziak and Plamondon II point out) when that view is based on our contemporary perceptions of the Columbia. Today, standing in a boat at Pillar Rock and with the aid of binoculars, one can easily see the bridge between Astoria, Oregon, and Megler, Washington—a distance of fourteen miles. Furthermore, for reasons discussed later, we can reasonably

Pillar Rock, photo by David Nicandri. In modern times, Pillar Rock is adorned with navigational equipment. The Point Ellice headland, which William Clark mistook for Cape Disappointment, is to the right of the rock beyond the low sand island created by dredge spoils in the middle distance of the river that were not present in 1805. Tongue Point, which Clark may have mistaken for Point Adams, is to the left of the rock. WSHS 2005.22.86.

---

assume that in Clark's time the bar of the Columbia, where the forces of river and sea met, was much farther inland than today—in the vicinity of the Astoria-Megler Bridge, whose northern terminus is Point Ellice. It would be difficult but not impossible at such a distance for a man with a telescope, standing in a boat at high tide, to see storm waves crashing on that bar.[16]

We should remember as well that Clark's impressions were based on sound as much as sight. Thwaites himself noted that, after a storm, one could probably hear ocean swells breaking on the Columbia's bar. November is one of the Northwest's stormiest months; Clark could indeed have heard this distant roar, just as he claimed, especially if it was carried on the prevailing westerly wind. In our noise-polluted modern world, it is easy to forget how far sound once traveled. Five months earlier, when Clark was approaching the Great Falls of the Missouri, he could hear their rumble twenty miles away.[17]

As intimated above, there remains the question of how to define the boundary between the Pacific and the Columbia. Is it a convenient but entirely imaginary line extending between Cape Disappointment and Point Adams (the orthodox proposition), or a physiographic reality where tidal forces subsume the river's flow (occurring much farther inland)? Broughton, for one, had an even more radical view of the matter.

Working in the service of Vancouver and therefore in contest with Gray, Broughton had obvious geopolitical motivation to diminish the American's prior entry into the Columbia. Nevertheless, he decided that the true mouth of the Columbia was not between Cape Disappointment and Point Adams; nor could it be readily defined by reference to either of two inland features, Baker Bay and Grays Bay, farther upstream. Broughton tells us that the lower estuary was from three to seven miles wide and laced with "shoals that extend from nearly side to side." To Broughton, the entire lower estuary constituted an oceanic inlet, the same conclusion that Meares had come to but with a different practical effect. This broad, shoal-laden stretch of water, wrote Broughton, "ought rather to be considered as a sound, than as constituting a part of the river." (In contemporary parlance, a sound was an oceanic [that is, saltwater] indent with many offshoots, most famously Puget Sound.) Broughton, in other words, regarded this shoaly lower reach not as a tidal extension of the Columbia but as an extension of the Pacific—an arm that by Broughton's definition stretched as far east as today's Skamokawa, Washington, several miles upstream of Pillar Rock.[18] One of the corps' enlisted men, Robert Frazer, held essentially the same view. In the prospectus to his never-published account of the journey, Frazer referred to "the Columbia river and the Bay [Broughton's "sound"] it forms on the Pacific Ocean."[19]

At least one subsequent journal entry makes clear that Clark harbored no doubts about the appropriateness of his journal entry for November 7. Both he and Lewis sometimes corrected (or edited for narrative effect) geographic findings based upon later observation or experience—but on this point Clark never wavered. On December 1, 1805, having by then traversed Cape Disappointment and a portion of the North Beach Peninsula, he wrote that it had been "24 days Since we arrived in Sight of the Great Western...

Ocian." Counting backwards on the calendar takes us to November 7 and the camp at Pillar Rock.[20] It should also be noted that Clark's composite map of the lower Columbia, completed at Fort Clatsop later that winter, includes the annotation "Ocean in View" adjacent to the Pillar Rock camp.[21]

Clark's most definitive reassertion can be found, by implication, in the now most underutilized source of information about the expedition—the paraphrase of the journals by Nicholas Biddle, published in 1814. We know Biddle consulted with Clark at length while drafting his narrative and that he was also assisted by Private George Shannon.[22] In Biddle's account for November 7, the river widened into "a kind of bay" just past a Wahkiakum Indian village of seven houses, at present-day Skamokawa. This, of course, is a simple restatement of Broughton's conclusion (as well as of Meares's). Biddle's version continues: "We had not gone far from the village when the fog cleared off, and we enjoyed the delightful prospect of the ocean—that ocean, the object of all of our labors, the reward of all our anxieties." Notwithstanding the interposition of Biddle's florid prose, if anything this text suggests the ocean came into view well upstream of the oft-disputed vantage of Pillar Rock. Biddle adds, "this cheering view exhilarated the spirits of all the party, who were still *more delighted on hearing* the distant roar of the breakers." Biddle tells us that from this location the voyagers traveled many more miles west until reaching a camp opposite Pillar Rock.[23]

A consecutive reading of these sources—Clark's field notes, journal, and course and distance records, and Biddle's narrative—shows that with each retelling of sighting the ocean at Pillar Rock, the story is strengthened, not diluted. Why would Clark (or his amanuensis Biddle) have been so aggressive in contradicting modernity's understanding of geographic fact?

The man-made changes at the mouth of the Columbia are one key to understanding Clark's supposed mistake. As noted, long after Lewis and Clark's day, Point Adams, on the Oregon shore, was extended by construction of a rock jetty some six miles long. Landfill on the Washington shore created a shorter jetty extending from Cape Disappointment.[24] The principal function of these jetties is to regularize a channel to and from the sea, which they accomplish, in effect, by moving the line of the ocean's confrontation with the river westward. Before the jetties, ocean storms surged much farther inland than they do today. Old-timers recall seeing the surf line at the approximate location of the present-day Astoria-Megler Bridge. And it is instructive to note that Megler, approximately a mile upriver from the bridge (and presently constituted as the Lewis and Clark National

Historical Park Dismal Nitch rest area/interpretive site), was established as the north-bank terminus for the old ferry service from Astoria precisely because one had to go that far upstream to avoid the worst the Columbia's bar could offer. Even so, there were many days when conditions kept the ferry from operating.[25]

A final, and perhaps most compelling, reason to believe Clark's statement is the principle of normative geographic expectations. Modern understanding of standard information, topographic or otherwise, often precludes seeing the world as the explorers saw it in real time. Clark's seemingly mysterious determination at Pillar Rock has to be appreciated from the river-level view of November 7, 1805, and his cartographic understanding of the terrain at the time. As the great nineteenth-century historian Francis Parkman stated, the historian "must study events in their bearings near and remote; in the character, habits and manners of those who took part in them. He must himself be, as it were, a sharer or spectator of the action he describes."[26]

Here we must return to the elusive—not to say illusive—Cape Disappointment. We know Lewis made a copy of Vancouver's map of the lower Columbia when preparing for the expedition in Philadelphia. We know too that the captains had Lewis's copy with them when they reached the lower Columbia, and that it confused and confounded them. Indeed, in both his journals and in dialogue with Biddle, Clark was emphatic in his dismissal of Vancouver's work.[27]

Vancouver's map of the estuary clearly conveyed Cape Disappointment's protuberance extending southward from the mainland in the form of a hook—a feature that Clark would later depict from his vantage at Station Camp. However, in this instance, the view of the world provided by a map in a library in Philadelphia had to be refracted through the lens of Clark's observations on the river in a dugout canoe. What Vancouver's chart did *not* accurately convey (let alone Lewis's copy of the same) was the prominence of Point Ellice protruding from the north shore. It is far more distinctive as a landmark when viewed from an upriver location such as Clark's at Pillar Rock. This is especially so from river level, which was Clark's vantage. Clark's entry for course and distance on November 8 makes clear that he regarded Cape Disappointment as the farthest landform to the west. But— and this is the crucial issue—the "Cape Disappointment" he thought he was observing was actually Point Ellice. In his entry Clark initially wrote "Cape disappointment," but from his perspective at Pillar Rock he could not have seen the real Cape Disappointment because Point Ellice obscures it. Sometime later, presumably after further exploration, he realized his error, crossed out "disappointment," and renamed it Point Distress. But in real time at Pillar Rock, Clark thought he was looking at Cape Disappointment, and he knew from Vancouver's map that the ocean lay immediately beyond it.[28]

Further substantiation of the perceived oceanic sighting—call it "the Point Ellice effect"—can be found elsewhere in the record for November 8. Whitehouse reports that, shortly after the explorers resumed their voyage, the view "continued as far as our Eyes could descern; & we expect that the River continues its width to the Mouth of it." Ordway comments, "we can See along distance a head" to the mouth of the river.[29] (He also noticed that the water was brackish, validating Broughton's conclusion.) It would be another ten days and twenty miles before Clark reached the "real" Cape Disappointment and gazed like a latter-day Balboa on the vast Pacific. To mark the occasion, he carved his name on a tree, along with the declaration that he had arrived there "by Land."[30]

NOTES

1. Gary E. Moulton, ed., *The Journals of the Lewis & Clark Expedition* (Lincoln: University of Nebraska Press, 1983–2001), 5: 362. Meriwether Lewis referred to "the corps of volunteers for North Western Discovery" in his journal entry for August 26, 1804. The more commonly used phrase "Corps of Discovery" never appears in the primary documentary record associated with Lewis and Clark. This phrasing was coined as a portion of the subtitle of Sergeant Patrick Gass's early, unauthorized account of the expedition, from whence it took its currency. See Stephen Dow Beckham et al., *The Literature of the Lewis and Clark Expedition: A Bibliography and Essays* (Portland, OR: Lewis & Clark College, 2003), 105. Lewis and Clark refer to an expedition for "North Western" discovery (or variations of this term) in other primary documents. See Donald Jackson, ed., *Letters of the Lewis and Clark Expedition with Related Documents: 1783–1854*, 2nd ed. (Urbana: University of Illinois Press, 1978), 1: 113, 210; 2: 549. Also, Moulton, *Journals*, 3: 14, 153, 170, 172n10; and 9: 231–32. The military term typically employed to refer to the command was "detachment," not "corps." The prime example is the orderly book containing the rules of military comportment and discipline. Instructively, the first "Detachment Order" at Camp River Dubois, on April 1, 1804, records the names of men selected for the "Perminent Detachment." A subsequent order at Wood River stated, "No man of the Detachment Shall leave Camp without permission from the Commanding officer present." Lewis retrospectively wrote of May 14, 1804, as the day "the detachment left the mouth of the River Dubois." After his court-martial, Private Moses Reed ran the gauntlet through the "Detachment." Moulton, *Journals*, 2: 187, 212, 412, and 488.

2. J. Richard Nokes, *Almost a Hero: The Voyages of John Meares, R. N., to China, Hawaii, and the Northwest Coast* (Pullman: Washington State University Press, 1998), 7–8, 61, 69–70.

3. W. Kaye Lamb, ed., *The Voyage of George Vancouver, 1791–1794* (London: Haklyut Society, 1984), 1: 76–79, 111–12; 2: 757–60. This is a modern edition of a work first published in London in 1798.

4. Moulton, *Journals*, 6: 58.

5. Stephen E. Ambrose, *Undaunted Courage: Meriwether Lewis, Thomas Jefferson, and the Opening of the American West* (New York: Simon & Schuster, 1996), 305; Reuben Gold Thwaites, *Original Journals of the Lewis and Clark Expedition, 1804–1806* (New York: Dodd, Mead, 1904–5), 3: 210n.

6. Rex Ziak, *In Full View* (Astoria, OR: Moffitt House Press, 2002), 186–89. Martin Plamondon II, *Lewis and Clark Trail Maps: A Cartographic Reconstruction* (Pullman: Washington State University Press, 2000–4), 3: 62.

7. Moulton, Journals, 6: 25, 29–30n19. Coffin Rock was destroyed early in the twentieth century to provide jetty rock at Cape Disappointment and Point Adams.

8. Moulton, *Journals*, 6: 26.

9. Ibid., 27. Moulton speculates that "Haley" may have been Samuel Hill, captain of the brig *Lydia* hailing from Boston, or William Shaler, captain of the brig *Lelia Bird*. On balance, Moulton favors Hill, who traded on the Columbia in April 1805, possibly as far upriver as the Cascades. Moulton, *Journals*, 6: 29n15.

10. Ibid., 31–32.

11. Ibid., 6: 31; 11: 390. The basis for Pillar Rock's name is only evident from the water. Over eons, the river currents have shaved its sides to create a narrow, pillar-like form.

12. Moulton, *Journals*, 6: 33.

13. Ibid., 58. Moulton believes that Codex H, in which these statements are found, was probably composed no earlier than April or May of 1806. Ibid., 2: 23, 25–26. Several well-known accounts of the Lewis and Clark Expedition have mistakenly attributed "*Ocian in view*! O! the joy" to Clark's elkskin-bound journal (that is, his field notes). See for example, Ambrose, *Undaunted Courage*, 305. Given the line's apparent spontaneity, this seems a logical choice, even though it is, in fact, the last of the three versions Clark wrote. The error can probably be traced to Bernard DeVoto's influential abridgment of the journals, where in a footnote he places this quote in "the notebook which he [Clark] kept on his knee to record courses and bearings." Following Thwaites's lead, DeVoto adds that Clark was "mistaken" about seeing the ocean from his camp near Pillar Rock. Bernard DeVoto, ed., *The Journals of Lewis and Clark* (Boston: Houghton Mifflin, 1953), 279n6.

14. Thwaites, *Journals*, 3: 210n; Moulton, *Journals*, 2: 7; 6: 35n. John Logan Allen, *Lewis and Clark and the Image of the American Northwest* (New York: Dover, 1991), 316. Ambrose, *Undaunted Courage*, 307–8. Ziak, *In Full View*, 186–89.

15. Ambrose, *Undaunted Courage*, 307–8.

16. Plamondon, *Trail Maps*, 3: 62. Plamondon II's discussion includes an analysis of how the horizon would have affected Clark's view. He states, "The earth's curvature perhaps is a consideration here. The distance from Pillar Rock to Point Ellice [the north terminus of the Astoria-Megler Bridge] is about 21 miles, with curvature figured at about 8 inches per mile for this area. Thus, the curvature would be approximately 14 feet. However, surface water elevations at Pillar Rock are not constant, but probably vary from about 3 to 6 feet above sea level. Clark sitting or standing in a canoe would add another 3 to 6 feet. Perhaps with his telescope he could see the distant ocean's high surf on the sand bars or possible storm swells up to a score or more feet high." Plamondon supports the view that the surf Clark saw and heard was breaking near Point Ellice, not at Cape Disappointment. My own map work tells me that the distance from Pillar Rock to Point Ellice is more like fourteen to fifteen miles, a distance that would lend further credibility to Clark's claim.

17. Thwaites, *Journals*, 3: 210n; Moulton, *Journals*, 4: 295, 297.

18. Vancouver, *Voyage*, 2: 752n. Notwithstanding Broughton's technically correct assertion that a river is constituted by fresh water, Vancouver states unequivocally that the Columbia was a "river Mr. Gray had discovered." Ibid., 691.

19. Jackson, *Letters*, 1: 345.

20. Ziak, *In Full View*, 189. In his journal entry for December 1, 1805, Clark wrote that the ocean "roars like a repeeted roling thunder and have rored in that way ever Since our arrival in its borders." Moulton, *Journals*, 6: 103.

21. Jackson, *Letters*, 1: 345. Moulton, *Journals*, 1: map 82; 6: 104.

22. Elliott Coues, *History of the Expedition under the Command of Lewis and Clark* (New York: Francis P. Harper, 1893), 1: xiii, lxxxiv. Coues's work is an edited and heavily annotated version of the Biddle edition, published in Philadelphia in 1814. See also Jackson, *Letters*, 2: 497–545. I am indebted to both Roger Wendlick and Robert Carriker for their insights on the continued value of Biddle, a source historians should not neglect.

23. Coues, *History*, 2: 702. Emphasis added. Biddle's interlineation found in Clark's journal entry for November 7 is consistent with the view that the ocean sighting occurred early in the day. Moulton, *Journals*, 6: 33.

24. Known locally as "jetties," these extensions are more than just piles of riprap. The South Jetty, which is more than six miles long, was constructed between 1885 and 1913. The North Jetty, some three miles long, was built between 1914 and 1917. The buildup of sediment and vegetation around these structures eventually created new land mass. As a result of these changes, the width of the Columbia's mouth—the span between Cape Disappointment and Point Adams—is about a mile, compared to three miles in Lewis and Clark's era. Plamondon, *Trail Maps*, 3: 62–63.

25. Harold Lampi, face-to-face conversation, March 7, 2002. Mr. Lampi was born in 1917 and lived most of his life in Clatsop County, Oregon.

26. Francis Parkman, *The Oregon Trail*, E. N. Feltskog, ed. (Madison: University of Wisconsin Press, 1969), 28a.

27. Jackson, *Letters*, 2: 540–41. Moulton, *Journals*, 1: 16n; 6: 47n3, 50. Very likely, the perceived deficiencies in Vancouver's geography owed as much to Lewis's "haisty manner" in making his copy. Jackson, *Letters*, 1: 53. Stephen Beckham writes that Lewis made this copy of Vancouver's map because the composite map made for the expedition by Nicholas King provided no details about the mouth of the river. Beckham speculates that when Clark "could not See any Island in the mouth of this river as laid down by Vancouver" he was misled by Lewis's handiwork, the latter having misinterpreted the placement of a sandbar for an island inside the capes. Moulton, *Journals*, 6: 50; Beckham, *Literature*, 41. However, it's also possible that Lewis mistook the cartographic symbol of an anchorage in the ocean outside the capes for an island. Vancouver's master map of the western coast of North America from Prince William Sound to San Diego only employs the anchorage symbol once, and very indistinctly, off the mouth of the Columbia River. Its inclusion may have been unintended, since a later edition of the map published in the 1801 octavo edition of Vancouver's account deleted the symbol. Alternatively, Lewis may have hurriedly copied Vancouver's section map of the northern tip of Vancouver Island to Cape Lookout on today's Oregon coast, which shows a penumbra or intimation of an island to the ocean side of Point Adams. It is this chart that contains an inset view of the map titled "Entrance of Columbia River." Lamb, *Voyage*, 1: xiv, back pocket.

28. Moulton, *Journals*, 6: 35, 52. Some have suggested that Lewis and Clark may have harbored additional oceanic expectations. As Rex Ziak has pointed out, preparing for a ceremonial arrival at the end of a voyage was a well-established exploratory tradition. In the few preceding days, the explorers had gotten underway early, but they broke camp late on November 8, "haveing Changed our Clothing." According to Ziak, the buckskin-clad explorers, expecting to find a naval ship, may have changed into uniform in order to properly greet its captain. Such an expectation is suggested by Joseph Whitehouse's journal entry for November 7, which says that Indians reported "vessells lying at the Mouth of this River." There could also be a simpler explanation. As related in the Biddle narrative, "It rained this morning [November 8], and having changed the clothing which had been wet during yesterday's rain, we did

not set out till nine o'clock." Subsequent and repeated references during the ensuing week about the party's deteriorated leather clothing would be consistent with this interpretation, especially in view of John Ordway's assertion that the party broke camp on the morning of the November 8 "as us[u]al." Ziak, *In Full View*, 9; Moulton, *Journals*, 6: 35, 39, 42–43, 47; 9: 251; 11: 390; Coues, *History*, 2: 702, 710, 720. Lewis retained possession of his officer's coat until March 17, 1806, when it was traded for a canoe just before leaving Fort Clatsop. Clark traded his for horses at The Dalles on April 20. Moulton, *Journals*, 6: 426; 7: 147. I am indebted to Roger Daniels, who took Roger Wendlick and me in his boat to see this part of the Columbia from Clark's river-level perspective.

29. Moulton, *Journals*, 9: 251; 11: 390.
30. Moulton, *Journals*, 6: 62. Entry for November 18, 1805. Clark's exact words are "here Capt Lewis myself & Severl. of the men marked our names day of the month & by Land &c. &c." Clark's more famous graffito—his name followed by the ringing phrase "By Land. U. States in 1804 & 1805"—was carved December 3 on a pine tree at Point William, on the Oregon side of the estuary. Ibid., 106. Presumably, the wording of his November 18 carving was substantially similar, and perhaps identical, to his carving of December 3.

CHAPTER 6

MERIWETHER LEWIS:

THE SOLITARY HERO

Having sighted an opening to the Pacific Ocean on November 8, 1805, members of the Lewis and Clark Expedition expected that one more day of travel would take them to the end of their westward voyage. In a turn of events reminiscent of Greek mythology, the detachment became marooned for the better part of a week at a location William Clark fittingly named "dismal nitch." After days of pummeling by the tempestuous weather, on November 14 Meriwether Lewis jumped ship, in a manner of speaking, and with a few other men rounded "Point Distress," a wave-tossed promontory that had kept the party place bound. Clark and the bulk of the party were left exposed to the elements back at the "nitch." Lewis's departure begs for scrutiny and doing so sheds considerable light upon the actual working relationship between the two men, in contrast to the bromides frequently offered about their co-captaincy.

Consider first Lewis's professed "object" in this undertaking. Since he was not keeping a journal at this point, per Clark his intention was to "examine if any white men were below within our reach." This explanation strains credulity. John Colter had just returned from the bay around "Point Distress" with Alexander Willard and George Shannon and conveyed the news that no traders or explorers were to be found. Colter hardly would have missed sighting ships around the point if there had been any. Private Joseph White-house said Lewis ventured off to visit the Indian village Colter saw at the mouth of the river—abandoned at the time—an even less credible scenario.[1]

There is a more plausible explanation for Lewis's evacuation from Dismal Nitch. (From this point forward I will use the capitalization of the site's name employed by the National Park Service in their steward-ship role.) Clark's journal entries, which form the predominant record of transactions from the time the expedition left the Nez Perce villages, inevitably favor his own activities in terms of their visibility. Notwithstanding this bias, from the time of Lewis's gastronomic sickness that literally laid him low on the Clearwater River, he rarely figured in the Columbia River story; that is, until November 14 at Dismal Nitch. Lewis's maneuver was grounded neither in the quest for the safety of the party nor an ethnographic inquiry. His motivation was narrow and purely personal. Colter's report that he, Willard, and Shannon had proceeded on along a sandy beach on the Columbia River side of Cape Disappointment risked that someone other than Lewis might be credited with the ultimate moment of discovery—reaching the Pacific and that first dramatic and completely open view of the ocean. Lewis had nearly all the other previous moments of discovery to himself. He was the first to see the Great Falls of the Missouri, and he had that legendary first glimpse into the Columbia country from the crest of the Continental Divide. Was an enlisted man going to perhaps claim that he beat Lewis to the western edge of the continent? In short, Lewis developed a case of what mountaineers call "summit fever."

Several clues substantiate this thesis. First, there is the curious phrasing Clark used to describe Lewis leading an advance party out of Dismal Nitch. Contrary to the usual practice of characterizing all major decisions through the use of the semantically inclusive "we," Clark states forthrightly that "Capt Lewis concluded" on this course of action. Second, there is the evidence embedded in a note Lewis later posted at Fort Clatsop, just prior to its abandonment in March 1806. Lewis's stated hope was that some "civilized person" might stumble upon the fort with his note still attached to its walls. Thereby the "informed world" would learn of the expedition that was "sent out by the government of the U' States." In this missive, Lewis explained that the party penetrated the continent by way of the Missouri and Columbia Rivers, "to the discharge of the latter into the Pacific Ocean, where they arrived on the *14th* November 1805" (emphasis added). This date was misleading on two counts. First, the great preponderance of the party on November 14 remained marooned east of Point Distress. Clark and the bulk of the detachment would not successfully depart Dismal Nitch for another day. Second, the Colter party rounded Point Distress, the last impediment to westward travel, on November 13.[2]

Lewis habitually employed this modus operandi throughout the expedition. It was no coincidence that Lewis was the first to see the Great Falls of the Missouri or the Continental Divide; he engineered those moments.

Clark's Dismal Nitch, by Roger Cooke (2003). In this pictorialization, we see three members of the expedition try to land a canoe while others struggle to set up camp in a storm. When Lewis jumped ahead to reach the Pacific Ocean as part of a seemingly calculated plan to put himself in the historical spotlight, Clark was marooned at this site with the bulk of the party. Courtesy of the Washington State Historical Society. WSHS 2005.22.66.

As Lewis & Clark College Professor Stephen Dow Beckham phrases it, Lewis "was quick to…dash for the prizes of discovery." Clay Jenkinson was the first scholar to note this tendency, observing that "Lewis took command at critical moments in the Expedition. He seems to have wanted to make the great discoveries of the Expedition alone." Lewis, Jenkinson writes, was a man "who struck poses."[3]

With most explorers, this penchant for egotism would not have presented much of a problem. Lewis, however, had a co-commander. The lore of the expedition holds that the captains always saw eye to eye. There were, in truth, no overt disturbances in what Gary E. Moulton terms "their remarkably harmonious relationship," and from this he concluded, "Lewis apparently treated Clark as…a partner whose abilities were complementary to his own." However, a deconstruction of the journals proves that Clark occasionally was disappointed by Lewis's behavior and possibly annoyed by it.[4]

From the beginning of the venture, Clark was disadvantaged by his relationship to Lewis. Clark shared in the command of the expedition,

Jenkinson writes, "by virtue of Meriwether Lewis's magnanimity rather than in actual rank." Lewis had failed to deliver on Clark's promotion to captain. This resulted in both men having to pretend Clark shared Lewis's rank. Consequently, as the second man in, it should not surprise us that Clark would have been, as James Holmberg states, "very conscious of titles, rank, and his pride." Clark later reminded Nicholas Biddle that in rank and command he was *equal in every point of view*" (emphasis in the original).[5]

When considered in conjunction with the larger body of Clark's crafty edits, demurrals, and disavowals in his own record, plus those he later embedded in Lewis's journals, his post-expeditionary comment to Biddle was tantamount to a protest. Clark was insistent that posterity not see his work in the field as that of a second in command or a junior officer even if, in practical reality, his rank was lower than Lewis's, as those in power in the nation's capital would have known too well. Tellingly, Clark's first expressed concern after learning of Lewis's death was to ask rhetorically, "what will become of *my*" corrected to "*his* paprs" (emphasis added). Clark had his own sense of ownership about the expedition and he knew the journals Lewis was carrying when he died were essential to history's appreciation of their joint venture.[6]

Clark occasionally was able to partially correct or otherwise recalibrate Lewis's record so as to more accurately reflect his contributions to the expedition. He never had access to certain documents (for example, manuscripts other than the journals) and when Lewis alone controlled those records there is no doubt about whose expedition it was. In a private letter to his mother written shortly before the expedition departed Fort Mandan in the spring of 1805, Lewis described having "arrived at this place…with the party under *my* command" (emphasis added). Excluding Clark may have been understandable if not excusable while writing to a close family member. However, Lewis later *published* a prospectus for the forthcoming account of travels and took credit not only for the prospective narrative but also the master map, work that had always been Clark's specialty. This map was to be compiled "from the collective information of the best informed travellers through the various portions of that region, and corrected by a series of several hundred celestial observations, made by Captain Lewis during *his* late tour" (emphasis added). This was double diminution of Clark's role: Lewis deigned to correct Clark while at the same time minimize his primary contribution. It was precisely this hauteur that David McKeehan skewered in defense of his right to publish Sergeant

Patrick Gass's journal in the face of Lewis's opposition to that unauthorized account of the expedition.[7]

Though the expedition's journals have the surface appearance of being an empirical chronology of events, they are, often as not, autobiography. In her explication of the exploratory genre, Barbara Belyea distinguishes between the narrative form of "the 'I' who writes and the 'me' who is written about." Inevitably, the explorer as writer becomes "the main textual subject." Though this narrative phenomenon was normative for explorers, Lewis took it to extremes. Consider, for example, Lewis's famous description of the scene when the expedition departed Fort Mandan. First, Lewis explicitly referred to Columbus and James Cook and, as previously discussed, then secretly drew upon Alexander Mackenzie via his expropriation of the term "darling project." Next he introduced the excitement associated with entering "a country at least two thousand miles in width, on which the foot of civillized man had never trodden." Lewis then wrote: "I could but esteem this moment of *my* departure as among the most happy of my life" (emphasis added). Framing this sentence, Lewis consciously struck over the word "our" before "departure," so this solitary construction was no accident. As Jenkinson says, here "Lewis's self-absorption is nearly complete." Lewis reduced a moment of common endeavor to what Thomas P. Slaughter calls a "singular and possessive accomplishment" that had the effect of reducing poor Clark "to the status of crew." Slaughter maintains that the ethos of exploration required of Lewis that he pose as the "singular hero." Indeed, departing from Fort Mandan Lewis effectively edited Clark out of the narrative. Actually, it was even starker than that. A year earlier, when the expedition left the Wood River campsite of 1803–4 on the Mississippi River, Lewis wrote himself into a story when in fact he was not with the party on the first leg up the Missouri. He joined it later at St. Charles by going overland from St. Louis.[8]

As Jenkinson avers, "at the critical moments of the Expedition, Lewis pushes the rest of the company out of his consciousness."[9] Thus, Lewis's jumping ahead of Clark and leaving him at Dismal Nitch was a calculated stratagem in keeping with a tendency visible from the very beginning of the "collaboration" with Clark, aimed at putting himself in the historical spotlight.

Consider, then, Clark's plight. He had regular access to Lewis's reflective journal during those stretches when he was making what is often referred to as his so-called verbatim copy. Thus, during the course of the expedition Clark had to occasionally bear the indignity of reading how

Lewis constructed this posed narrative. Only through the fateful turn in Lewis's post-expeditionary life did Clark secure editorial control over his associate's expeditionary record.

The first notable instance of Lewis's questing for glory west of Fort Mandan occurred during the approach to the Yellowstone River's confluence with the Missouri—what Lewis termed a "long wished for spot," a common trope in exploration literature—several miles east of the present-day border between North Dakota and Montana. Unfavorable winds had been retarding the progress of the watercraft for several days in late April 1805. Knowing from the reports of the hunters out ahead that the Yellowstone was not far away, Lewis determined to avoid any further "detention." He proceeded ahead by land with a few men "to the entrance of that river" to make the astronomical observations that would fix its position, "which I hoped to effect by the time that Capt. Clark could arrive with the party." When Clark finally caught up, they quibbled a bit over the best location for the emplacement of a future trading post.[10]

Lewis's most famous discovery was the Great Falls of the Missouri. The Hidatsa told the captains that reaching this feature was the sure sign that they were on the correct route to the Columbia. This point was so axiomatic in the expedition's understanding of western geography that it served as the solution to the quandary faced by the party at the surprising appearance of the Marias River. Then and there Pierre Cruzatte and the other men in the detachment forced the captains' hands on the question of which branch of the river was the route to its headwaters. Lewis complained that, contrary to his and Clark's opinion, Cruzatte, "an old Missouri navigator...had acquired the confidence of every individual of the party...that the N. fork [the Marias] was the true genuine Missouri." Indeed, the men were "so determined in this beleif, and wishing that if we were in an error to be able to detect it and rectify it as soon as possible it was agreed between Capt. C. and myself that one of us should set out with a small party by land up the South fork [the Missouri] and continue our rout up it untill we found the falls."[11]

Tensions now emerged within the joint command because of what Slaughter calls the conventions of exploration as a "solitary event." As Lewis phrased it in his approximately 1,400-word account about the decision at the Marias, "this expedition [in search of the falls and thus the true Missouri] I prefered undertaking as Capt. C [is the] best waterman &c. and determined to set out the day after tomorrow." Clark's corresponding report numbers less than two hundred words. Of Lewis's decision to jump ahead, he writes tersely about effecting a cache of one pirogue, tools, powder and lead, and as soon as "accomplished to assend the South fork." The absence of any nouns or pronouns in this last phrasing may be telling. His only mention of Lewis by name is to report that his co-commander was "a little unwell to day," and that he had to take "Salts &c." This would be the start of another pattern—Lewis becoming physically ill on those occasions when the fate of the expedition seemed to hang in the balance, which must be seen as equivalent in Lewis's mind to his prospective reputation as a solitary and heroic explorer. Lewis described his illness as "disentary."[12]

In Slaughter's view, "companions create narrative problems for the explorer." In Lewis's case, Clark's presence was merely the most obvious one. When Lewis "jumped ship" on his quest for the Great Falls and exploratory glory, George Drouillard, Joseph Field, George Gibson, and Silas Goodrich accompanied him. However, a few days later, when Lewis encountered the "sublimely grand spectacle," these men virtually disappear from the narrative. The experience with nature's wonders is Lewis's alone.[13]

Later that summer, once the expedition reached the Three Forks of the Missouri, the next great moment of discovery loomed—"seeing the head of the missouri yet unknown to the civilized world," as Lewis phrased it, and the Continental Divide from which it sprang. During this segment of the trip Clark had been proceeding ahead of the flotilla on land with the hunters, and he relished being in the vanguard. We know this from Lewis, who noted that "Capt C. was much fatiegued[,] his feet yet blistered and soar," yet he "*insisted* on pursuing his rout in the morning nor *weould he consent willingly* to my releiving him at that time by taking a tour of the same kind" (emphasis added). This remarkably revealing entry becomes even more interesting when posed with Lewis's next comment: "finding [Clark] anxious I readily consented to remain with the canoes." Something more than Clark just toughing it out is clearly at play here. Even Biddle sensed the tension and attempted to sanitize the account by substituting the more neutral "*deturmined*" for the vexatious "insisted" found in Lewis's original text.[14]

Clark's intention was "to proceed on in pursute of the Snake Indians," the gatekeepers to the Rocky Mountain passage. An encounter with the Shoshones would have insured Clark a central moment in the master narrative of the expedition's putative glories. Lewis, two days behind Clark, knew that his co-commander had "pursued the Indian road," had found an abandoned horse, and "saw much indian sign." Meanwhile, Lewis and the balance of the expedition labored in poling and hauling the canoes over the riffles in the riverbed.[15]

On July 25, Clark and his advance guard reached the Three Forks and proceeded up what he termed the "main North fork" (later to be called the Jefferson River). This fork, Clark wrote expectantly, "affords a great Deel of water and appears to head in the Snow mountains." Here was Clark's main chance. Lewis observed that on the basis of a note left for him at the Three Forks Clark was on a course "in the direction we were anxious to pursue." Unfortunately for Clark, his continued exertions in defiance of blistered and bruised feet (the result of repeated exposure to prickly pear cactus) and a somewhat straitened diet (not so much from supply but opportunity to eat), combined with oppressive midsummer heat, made him sick. Suffering from a high fever and chills, constipated, and losing his appetite altogether because of the fatigue brought on by his vigorous march ahead of Lewis and the canoes, Clark turned back to the Three Forks, exhausted. There he met up with Lewis coming up from behind with the main party.[16]

For two days beginning July 28, 1805, Lewis doctored Clark at the Three Forks. Lewis had "a small bower or booth erected" for Clark's comfort because the "leather lodge when exposed to the sun is excessively hot." Clark's fever dissipated slowly and though the recovery had begun, he complained "of a general soarness in all his limbs." Lewis, however, was anxious to get going. On the July 30, the detachment broke camp, with Lewis leading that pivotal vanguard of hunters on foot, and Clark and the voyageurs bringing up the rear. After only one day into this arrangement, Lewis admitted having "waited at my camp very impatiently for the arrival of Capt. Clark and party." Becoming by his own admission "uneasy" with this pattern, Lewis determined on the next day to go "in quest of the Snake Indians." Lewis took Drouillard, Toussaint Charbonneau, and Sergeant Gass on this mission. As had happened to Lewis when he jumped ahead of Clark in pursuit of the Great Falls, once again the excitement of becoming the exploratory hero brought on "a slight desentary." Lewis packed away a sheaf of papers with which to record notes that might be adapted into a narrative worthy of posterity's reading.[17]

The day Lewis leapt ahead, August 1, happened to be Clark's birthday. Clark reported tersely: "Capt. Lewis left me at 8 oClock"—that is, left him behind to slog up the gravelly bed of the Jefferson River with the canoes. Clark's physical problems mounted when his ankle swelled. One day ahead of the main party, Lewis reached the forks of the Jefferson and determined that the tributary stream known today as the Beaverhead River, with its warmer water and gentler flow, was the more navigable route. Lewis deduced that the Beaverhead "had it's source at a greater distance in the mountains and passed through an opener country than the other." Lewis left a note for Clark on a pole at the Jefferson forks instructing him on the recommended route for the canoes should he not return to that spot before the main party got there.[18]

Once a few miles up the Beaverhead fork of the Jefferson, Lewis could see that this watershed headed in a "gap formed by it in the mountains." With that promising prospect in front of him, Lewis wrote: "I did not hesitate in beleiving the [Beaverhead] the most proper for us to ascend." Better yet, "an old indian road very large and plain leads up this fork." This was the path to the Shoshones, the Continental Divide, waters that drained to the Pacific, and to glory.[19]

Down below, Clark was barely able to walk. The "poleing men" and those hauling the canoes were "much fatigued from their excessive labours… verry weak being in the water all day." After his initial reconnaissance of the Beaverhead, Lewis returned to the forks of the Jefferson River expecting to find "Capt. C. and the party…on their way up." Lewis was dismayed upon reaching the forks because he discerned that Clark had not taken the recommended route up the Beaverhead, but instead had opted for one to the northwest known today as the Big Hole River. Lewis sent Drouillard after him and later "learnt from Capt. Clark that he had not found the note which I had left for him at that place and the reasons which had induced him to ascend" the more rapid northwesterly branch. In a comic twist, a beaver had gnawed down the post holding Lewis's directions, which caused near disastrous consequences for poor Clark, who had simply followed the stream with the greatest flow—a fundamental hydrological principle that had always guided the expedition.[20]

Lewis's journal referred to this rather pointedly as Clark's "mistake in the rivers." Clark's spirits were as dampened as the baggage that had been under his care while ascending the Big Hole. In his journal, Lewis charmed himself with his narrative on naming the tributaries of the Jefferson River the "Wisdom" and the "Philanthropy, in commemoration of two of those cardinal virtues" of the president who dispatched them. Clark included nary a word about this fanciful stuff in his account of that dismal day. He rather sparingly reported instead about Drouillard catching up with him with the news that the route he was on "was impractiabl" and that "all the

Indian roades" led up the fork that Lewis had scouted. Clark, writing with a tinge of resignation, noted that he "accordingly Droped down to the forks where I met with Capt Lewis & party." Clark's sore ankle was "much wors than it has been," the physical pain compounding the embarrassment of having taken the wrong turn.[21]

The captains traveled together for two days up the Beaverhead fork of the Jefferson but by the end of the second, August 8, 1805, Lewis had had enough. He decided to "leave the charge of the party, and the care of the lunar observations to Capt. Clark" while he would proceed ahead the next day "with a small party to the source of the principal stream of this river and pass the mountains to the Columbia." The boil or cyst on Clark's ankle had "discharged a considerable quantity of matter" but it was still swollen and left him in "considerable pain," Lewis reported. The morning Lewis forged ahead, as Clark stated, "to examine the river above, find a portage if possible, also the Snake Indians," he added a most poignant observation: "I Should have taken this trip had I have been able to march."[22]

Clark's declaration is one of the most suggestive of any to be found in the million words in the journals of the expedition. It exudes chagrin about not being able to make contact with the Shoshones, and more particularly the Columbia River. Furthermore, one can intuit from his text that after Lewis's previous forays in pursuit of the Yellowstone River and the Missouri's Great Falls that Clark, for certain, and maybe both captains had concluded it was Clark's turn for glory. Elliott Coues was the first to observe that "Captain Clark was sadly disappointed at not being able to take the lead in the trip." More recently Stephen E. Ambrose said, "Clark wanted to lead" this reconnaissance, but in the end it instead proved to be Lewis's "most important mission." This, of course, gets to the heart of what was bothering Clark.[23]

Fate, in the form of an ulcerous sore, denied Clark the opportunity to be the first over the Continental Divide. At the moment Lewis abandoned Clark on the headwaters of the Missouri, Clark's rendezvous with destiny dissipated. Everyone in the party saw the consequences. As Sergeant John Ordway put it, Captain Lewis had gone on ahead "to make discoveries."[24]

Three weeks later, when the expedition was about to depart the company of the Lemhi Shoshone, Lewis let slip his characteristic outlook when he referred, once again, to resuming what he called "my voyage." Such egotism has been an easy target from as early as 1807 in the form of McKeehan's broadside in defense of his client, Sgt. Gass, wanting to publish an account of the voyage. Nevertheless, Lewis was not completely oblivious about his obligations to his friend and co-commander. Lewis named the Clark Fork of the Columbia after him, in partial reciprocation for Clark having named the Lewis (Snake) River. But where Lewis had, in fact, been the first to the Columbia's waters, Clark's honor was a mere gratuity. As Coues observed, Clark had not been the proverbial "first white man" on the waters named for him; or at least, no more so than any other man in the expedition, since he was with the entire party when it crossed into the Bitterroot/Clark Fork watershed.[25]

Throughout his joint venture with Lewis, Clark's modesty shone through, a virtue not easily lent to his partner. Years later, Clark grumbled about the predicament in which his co-captain had put him, referencing the "trouble and expence" of getting the journals into print. Clark, in the end, was up to this task. Possessing the advantage of having been the more diligent, if less florid, journal keeper, he repeatedly exercised the option of editing the expedition's documentary record in order to create a more accurate account of events. In this respect, Clark was both the expedition's first historian, and later the historian's friend, for the benefit of posterity. We are left to wonder, had Lewis lived to write his account, how would Clark have fared in that narrative?[26]

──────── N O T E S ────────

1. Gary E. Moulton, ed., *The Journals of the Lewis & Clark Expedition* (Lincoln: University of Nebraska Press, 1983–2001), 6: 46, 11: 393.

2. Moulton, *Journals*, 6: 47, 429.

3. Stephen Dow Beckham, *Lewis and Clark: From the Rockies to the Pacific* (Portland, OR: Graphics Arts Center, 2002), 64; Clay S. Jenkinson, *The Character of Meriwether Lewis: "Completely Metamorphosed" in the American West* (Reno, NV: Marmarth Press, 2000), 9, 50.

4. Moulton, *Journals*, 2: 6.

5. Jenkinson, *Lewis*, 53; James J. Holmberg, ed., *Dear Brother: Letters of William Clark to Jonathan Clark* (New Haven, CT: Yale University Press, 2002), 72; Donald Jackson, ed., *Letters of the Lewis and Clark Expedition with Related Documents, 1783–1854* (Urbana: University of Illinois Press, 1978), 2: 571.

6. Holmberg, *Dear Brother*, 218.

7. Jackson, *Letters*, 1: 222, 2: 396. See Ibid., 2: 399–407 for McKeehan's critique of Lewis. John Logan Allen, *Lewis and Clark and the Image of the American Northwest* (New York: Dover, 1991), 373n39. The monument at Lewis's gravesite in Tennessee, erected in 1848, cites Lewis as "Commander of the Expedition" to Oregon. Elliott Coues, ed., *History of the Expedition under the Command of Lewis and Clark* (New York: Francis P. Harper, 1893), 1: lx.

8. Barbara Belyea, ed., *Columbia Journals: David Thompson*, reprint ed. (Seattle: University of Washington Press, 1998), xvii; Moulton, *Journals*, 4: 9–10; Jenkinson, *Lewis*, 55; Thomas P. Slaughter, *Exploring Lewis and Clark: Reflections on Men and Wilderness* (New York: Alfred A. Knopf, 2003), 36, 53.

9. Jenkinson, *Lewis*, 99.

10. Moulton, *Journals*, 4: 66, 70, 77.

11. Ibid., 4: 271.
12. Slaughter, *Exploring Lewis and Clark*, 29; Moulton, *Journals*, 4: 271, 274–75.
13. Slaughter, *Exploring Lewis and Clark*, 29; Moulton, *Journals*, 4: 283.
14. Moulton, *Journals*, 4: 416–17.
15. Ibid., 4: 418, 423–24.
16. Ibid., 4: 427–28, 433n9, 436.
17. Ibid., 4: 436, 5: 8, 11, 17–18, 24–25.
18. Ibid., 5: 29, 40.
19. Ibid., 5: 44–45.
20. Ibid., 5: 43, 47, 52.
21. Ibid., 5: 53–55. Ironically, Clark's route up the Big Hole River could have ended up being more productive than Lewis's. Clark's led to the relatively benign grade followed by modern highway I-15 over Deer Lodge Pass (elevation 5,902 feet) and into the Clark Fork River Basin, draining to Missoula, Montana, in the vicinity of Traveler's Rest. Lewis's path took the expedition over both Lemhi Pass (elevation 7,373 feet) and Lost Trail Pass (elevation 7,014 feet) before reaching Traveler's Rest. This proves, once again, Clark's superior geographic instincts.
22. Ibid., 5: 59, 62–63.
23. Coues, *History*, 2: 471n22; Stephen E. Ambrose, *Undaunted Courage: Meriwether Lewis, Thomas Jefferson, and the Opening of the American West* (New York: Simon & Schuster, 1996), 262, 264.
24. Moulton, *Journals*, 9: 199.
25. Ibid., 5: 173; Coues, *History*, 2: 584–85n13.
26. Holmberg, *Dear Brother*, 236.

CHAPTER 7

PURE WATER:

LEWIS'S HOMESICKNESS AT FORT CLATSOP

O n the morning of January 1, 1806, Meriwether Lewis "was awoke at an early hour by the discharge of a volley of small arms, which was fired by our party in front of our quarters to usher in the new year." With that line, Lewis resumed maintenance of his journal for the balance of the expedition's stay at Fort Clatsop, having stopped writing a connected narrative the previous fall. The gap in Lewis's journal during the crescendo of his venture to the Pacific Ocean (September 23–December 31, 1805) is noteworthy in itself and often remarked upon in the literature of the expedition, but it is perhaps explained by the contents of the next full sentence. The detachment's "repast of this day," he wrote, "tho' better than that of Christmass, consisted principally in the anticipation of the 1st day of January 1807, when in the bosom of our friends we hope to participate in the mirth and hilarity of the day, and when with the zest given by the recollection of the present, we shall completely, both mentally and corporally, enjoy the repast which the hand of civilization has prepared for us." In the meantime, Lewis reported, "we were content with eating our boiled Elk and wappetoe, and solacing our thirst with our only beverage *pure water.*"[1]

Lewis here took the liberty of speaking for everyone's sentiment at the moment, but given the festivity implied in the firing of the volley he may have been speaking mostly for himself. In any event, he inscribed thereby one of the more revealing passages among the millions of words he, William Clark, and the other journal keepers penned in the course of the expedition. A surefire indicator that this passage was considered a little too revelatory is proved by Nicholas Biddle's editorial decision to delete this sentimentality from his composite account of the journals published in 1814. Biddle elides over Lewis's emotional outbreak thusly: "for though we have reason to be gayer than we were at Christmas, our only dainties are the boiled elk and wappatoo, enlivened by draughts of pure water." Elliott Coues, in his annotation of the original publication issued in 1893, with Lewis's original manuscript journal in front of him, also passed over the captain's glum text.[2]

Expressions of homesickness were not unheard of in exploratory accounts. The most salient came during the first (1768–71) of Captain James Cook's three epic voyages of global maritime exploration when his *Endeavour* exited Torres Strait and headed into the Arafura Sea between Australia and New Guinea. By that very act, that is, confirming that New Guinea was not a northern projection of the continental mass of what earlier Dutch explorers had called New Holland, the discovery phase of that voyage concluded. Thereupon, Joseph Banks (1743–1820), the expedition's chief naturalist, noticed an immediate change in the mood of the crew. Just weeks after Cook had engineered a seemingly providential recovery of the ship on the Great Barrier Reef, Banks reported: "The greatest part of them were now pretty far gone with the longing for home which the Physicians have gone so far as to esteem a disease under the name of Nostalgia; indeed I can find hardly any body in the ship clear of its effects but the Captn[,] Dr Solander and myself, indeed we three have pretty constant employment for our minds which I beleive to be the best if not the only remedy for it."[3]

John C. Beaglehole, the mid-twentieth century editor of both Cook's and Banks's journals, noted that this was one of the first recorded uses of the term "nostalgia," a neologism coined earlier by Swiss scholar Johannes Hofer (1669–1752) in his 1688 doctoral dissertation. Today the word connotes a benign fondness for happier times and "the good old days," but Banks's usage is drawn from its original application as a medical label describing an acute and debilitating condition closely allied to melancholy and depression. The word's etymological roots in Greek essentially stand for the pain of being away from home. The term's novelty made John Hawkesworth, the editor of Cook's published account who relied on both the captain's journal and that of Banks, wary of using this idiomatic expression in print. But more to the point, Banks was unmistakably conveying the view that, psychologically at least, the expedition was effectively over for everyone except for himself, his assistant Daniel Solander, and Cook. Beaglehole pointedly observed in his introduction to Banks's journal that the *Endeavour* crew was "becoming bored with the voyage. They were not starved, they were well looked after, their health, at the end of two years out from home, was excellent; not one man had died of sickness—an astonishing feat for any captain. What they wanted, however, was not the consolation of good health or reflections on the excellence of their commander's administration, but a known port, the sight of European faces, and a great deal of fresh food of the kind that Europeans recognized as food. After that they wanted a conventional voyage across known seas homeward."[4]

A close look at the journals for all three of Cook's voyages indicates that the Banks/Beaglehole two-year marker ascribed to the first expedition holds up for the two voyages that followed as well. There was a lot of grumbling on *Resolution* during the austral summer of 1774 when Cook steered the ship toward the Antarctic Circle for the second time during his second year in search of *Terra Australis Incognita*. For this journey the team of Johann Reinhold Forster and his son George replaced Banks and Solander as the principal naturalists, but here even the men of science succumbed to the nostalgic malaise. George Forster stated the "long continuance in these cold climates began now to hang heavily on our crew, especially as it banished all hope of returning home this year, which had hitherto supported their spirits. At first a painful despondence, owing to the dreary prospect of another year's cruise to the South, seemed painted in every countenance." Forster said Cook's crew "resigned themselves to their fate" by degrees until their outlook took on the cast of "a kind of sullen indifference."[5]

The discontent aboard *Resolution* took such forms as grumbling over the state of provision, which situation Cook was forced to redress all the while driving the ship toward its highest southern latitude southwest of Cape Horn. It was upon reaching 71°10' S that Cook inscribed one of the most memorable lines in the history of exploration. He referred to having gone not only "farther than any other man has been before me, but as far as I think it possible for man to go."[6] This line later inspired both *Star Trek*'s Gene Roddenberry and the Apollo moon program's Neil Armstrong.

When Cook turned from the ice his officers, if not everyone on board, thought *Resolution* would surely aim for the Cape of Good Hope, thereby concluding the second voyage's discovery phase. Cook, however, had other plans and determined on conducting a third season of high-latitude voyaging, this time in the Atlantic Ocean. He was temporarily able to assuage the sentiments of his crew and its scientific detachment about an extension of the voyage into another year with the enticing prospect of a "Winter within the Tropicks" and all such a sojourn portended climatically and sexually. George Forster wrote that the prospect of "enjoying the excellent refreshments which those islands afford, entirely revived our hopes, and made us look on our continuance on the western side of Cape Horne [sic] with some degree of satisfaction." Nevertheless, the Forsters were soon grousing again about Cook's route and timetable and the fatigue brought on by a long voyage. Nostalgic yearnings for home were having a pronounced negative effect on group psychology which resulted in an increasing number and intensity of fracases his crew was having beachside.[7]

The same pattern of disaffection is apparent on Cook's final voyage (1776–80) in search of the Northwest Passage. This expedition reached its two-year point on the final approach to the edge of Arctic ice pack, the apex of the venture's discovery phase, which occurred in August 1778. Once again, following the pattern that Banks had first noted nearly a decade earlier, the combination of fatigue and a sense of anticlimax combined to create shipboard discord. There was another bout of grumbling over the state of provender; this time the men objected to Cook forcing them to eat walrus meat. A month later, in Norton Sound, on the way back through the Aleutians and eventually to Hawaii, there was murmuring over the supply of beer and grog. This was a mere prequel to an even angrier outburst about the quality of the beer Cook had brewed off the coast of Maui, behavior that Cook deemed nearly mutinous. And, most famously, there is Cook's own fate to consider. Historian Frank McLynn recently distilled two generations' worth of Cook historiography about the third voyage, which is usually seen through the lens of his death in Kealakekua Bay on the Big Island of Hawaii. He writes that "Cook was old and tired when he embarked…, no longer the man he used to be, increasingly cross-grained and short-fused and no longer up to the combined stresses of his Admiralty orders, dealing with hostile or recalcitrant Polynesians and the perils of the Pacific."[8] The thrust of McLynn's argument is that while Cook may have been able to work through the exhaustion on the earlier voyages, rededicating himself to the mission when others began pining for home, the strain of command eventually became too burdensome even for the greatest and most persevering navigator of the era.

In light of the Cook-voyages experiences and Banks's nostalgia theory, what then of Lewis at Fort Clatsop in January 1806? It may be argued that Lewis's resumption of his journal after a three-month hiatus represented a New Year's resolution to be more diligent. Furthermore, Lewis's renewal appears to be a direct application of Banks's "remedy" of "constant employment" of the mind. Of course, Lewis had a preceptor nearer at hand than Britain's Banks. His mentor and patron Thomas Jefferson, in many

John Webber, *Sea Horses*, in *A Voyage to the Pacific Ocean*, by James Cook and James King (London: G. Nicol and T. Cadell, 1784), atlas pl. 52. Walrus meat was one among many dietary experiments Captain Cook conducted. In this engraving from Webber's drawing, British seamen hunt walruses from boats in the Chukchi Sea above Bering Strait on Cook's final voyage. Courtesy of the Washington State Historical Society. WSHS 2011.0.60.3.40.

respects an American counterpart to Banks and the New World's principal exemplar of the Enlightenment, also insisted that a busy life was the best antidote to melancholia.[9]

Indeed, Lewis had few if any stretches of time where he was more productive in his cataloging of people, plants, and animals than the winter at Fort Clatsop. In short, to counteract poignant nostalgic pangs Lewis threw himself into one last burst of scientific endeavor. He may even have convinced himself that he could redeem himself as an expedition record-keeper by compensating at Fort Clatsop for his silences earlier in the journey. Nevertheless, as I have argued elsewhere,[10] Lewis was worn down by the burden of command and suffered a kind of slow-motion nervous breakdown, as reflected in his increasingly irritable manner and occasional suspension of good judgment on the return voyage.

It is also worthy of remark that on his way home Lewis barely avoided the fate that befell Cook in Hawaii twenty-seven years earlier. Lewis literally dodged a bullet aimed at him by a Blackfoot warrior on the upper Marias watershed in Montana and he came close to being accidentally killed by one of his own men later that summer of 1806. In a sense he was fortunate to return home at all to "the bosom of [his] friends," but, as has been well documented in the literature about the expedition and its aftermath, his problems were not over. The most troubling circumstance for Jefferson was the extension of a pattern established during the course of the expedition and amply evident in retrospect, namely Lewis's inability to produce a published narrative worthy of the standard largely established by Captain Cook. Lewis's field journal ended after he was shot on August 11, 1806, by Pierre Cruzatte. We don't hear from him again until his post-expeditionary missives.

Lewis and Clark returned to St. Louis "about 12 oClock" on September 23, 1806, looking, observed a local gentleman, like refugees from *Robinson Crusoe*. Lewis was anxious to get word to Jefferson on the fate of the mission as soon as possible, going so far as preparing drafts while still floating down the Missouri. Seemingly the first thing he did is send a messenger to the postmaster in Cahokia on the opposite side of the Mississippi asking that the mail be held there until noon the next day so it could include a letter to the president. According to Clark, he and Lewis "rose early" on September 24 and "Commencd wrighting our letters," one of which was specifically identified as intended for the commander-in-chief. Though dated the previous day, Lewis's letter to Jefferson, together with Clark's correspondence to friends and family in Kentucky, was dispatched to Cahokia in the care of the indispensable George Drouillard. If any more proof was necessary to document the fact that Drouillard was one of the captains' most-trusted members of the expedition, surely this is it.[11]

Though rich in detail and much analyzed in expedition historiography, for present purposes the operative portion of Lewis's report to the president from September 23 is this line: "The anxiety which I feel in returning once more to the bosom of my friends is a sufficient guarantee that no time will be unnecessarily expended in this quarter." Here Lewis replicates the nostalgic yearning for home expressed at Fort Clatsop almost ten months earlier. Lewis stipulated for Jefferson's benefit that he had delayed the mail "for the purpose of making you this haisty communication," which he further described as "laconic," that is, insufficiently detailed to do justice to the immense journey now finally completed.[12]

In fact, the document is lengthy and studied in its composition and personal expressiveness and is hardly inadequate. Keeping to his word, Lewis left St. Louis in late October, reaching Staunton, Virginia, by December 11 and the nation's capital on December 28. He had succeeded in reaching the "bosom" of his coterie of family and friends just three days shy of the pledge he had made along the Pacific coast a year earlier. Undoubtedly, the repast that the hand of Jefferson put before him at his semiannual White House reception on January 1, 1807, was splendid fare compared to the spoiled elk at Fort Clatsop. And Bordeaux invariably trumps water.

After resigning from the army on March 2, 1807, Lewis prepared a memorandum regarding his forthcoming account, which notice was published in the *National Intelligencer* on March 14. Partially intended to warn the reading public against spurious publications that might appear before his official report was issued, Lewis made another New Year's resolution, of a sort, promising that volume 1 of the anticipated three would be in print by January 1, 1808, a mere ten months distant. When the book failed to appear on schedule, Jefferson grew concerned. On July 17, 1808, he wrote Lewis complaining about not receiving "a line from you." Ostensibly, this was a prosaic reference to the lack of communication from the former captain, but we know it was the expedition report, already half a year late in appearing, that was at the forefront of the president's mind. "We have no tidings yet of the forwardness of your printer. I hope the first part [volume 1] will not be delayed much longer." Only three days earlier, on Bastille Day, Jefferson promised a Parisian friend, Bernard Lacépède, a copy of "Govr. Lewis's work, as it appears," which suggests that the president was expecting to ship one soon.[13]

As we know, Lewis hadn't made any progress on his manuscript and, after yet another year passed, Jefferson, now in a more agitated state, again raised the subject with Lewis. "I am very often applied to know," he wrote on August 16, 1809, "when your work will begin to appear; and I have so long promised copies to my literary correspondents in France, that I am almost bankrupt in their eyes. I shall be very happy to receive from yourself information of your expectations on this subject. Every body is impatient for it."[14] Lewis never responded to what would turn out to be Jefferson's last letter to him, if in fact he ever saw it. It often took upwards of a month for correspondence to reach St. Louis from the capital and Lewis left Missouri for Washington, DC, on August 25. Clark was under the impression that Lewis was headed east in order to finish the expeditionary account, but undoubtedly his first order of business once he got there was to contest the government's rejection of his request for reimbursement of expenses for relocating a Mandan chief to his homeland. This circumstance, in turn, caused Lewis to be harried by creditors who had loaned him money to engage in land speculation. It is conceivable that Clark could have forwarded Jefferson's letter to Lewis at Chickasaw Bluffs, today's Memphis (only 280 miles downstream from St. Louis), where he remained until September 29. If so, the tone of it, and Lewis's realization that his nonfeasance had mortified his patron and hero, probably contributed materially to the path of dissolution that led to his suicide early the next month.

Historians have long puzzled over Lewis's failure to publish but there is no scholarly consensus explaining it. The theories range from simple procrastination, dissolute tendencies, administrative distraction in St. Louis, or mental depression. In any event, as noted in chapter 3, the failure by modern students of the expedition to appreciate the fact that travel accounts were a part of a well-established literary tradition, with its own set of conventions drawing on implicit cultural norms, limits our ability to understand the operative contexts and narrative choices explorer-authors made to describe them. That is to say, travel literature contained standardized episodes and expressive idioms that were either explicitly prescribed or contained implied meanings for the benefit of the knowing reader. For that reason, travel writers borrowed from each other regularly because they operated in the belief that the reading public came to their texts expecting to encounter similar tropes, conventions, stories, and motifs. The specific circumstances—dates, places, people—were of course different, but the narrative sentiments were relatively commonplace. It was not unusual for authors to bemoan their inability to do justice to the sublimity of something they were attempting to describe or, as Lewis once put it, to "give to the enlightened world some just idea of this truly magnificent and sublimely grand object, which has from the commencement of time been concealed from the view of civilized man."[15]

By the same token, as an imaginative act we too can draw on that same literary tradition to provide ourselves meanings from it and apply them analogously. This, one might say, is what all of literature, fiction or non-fiction, does. Consider then, as a window of understanding into Lewis's yearnings for home, the emotional experiences described by Richard Henry Dana Jr. (1815–82) in his *Two Years Before the Mast*, originally published in 1840. In 1834 Dana left his studies at Harvard and signed on as a common seaman aboard the *Pilgrim*, a brig engaged by a New England firm to ply the California coast in the trade for hides. Eighteen months into the voyage a sister ship, the *California*, arrived with a packet of mail from Boston, unleashing a wave of emotions among Dana and his shipmates. Dana wrote of the seaman's "natural feeling for home and friends" and explained that "everyone away from home thinks that some great thing must have happened, while to those at home there seems to be a continued monotony and lack of incident."[16]

The *California*'s appearance signaled that his time in the Pacific was about to draw to a close and, according to Dana, it "put life into everything when we were getting under way." "One would have thought we were on our voyage home," Dana continued, "so near did it seem to us, though there were yet three months for us on the coast," including the chain of ports he and his mates called on in regular sequence. "As I bade good-bye to each successive place, I felt as though one link after another were struck from the chain of my servitude." So wrote a man feeling imprisoned by serial visits to trading stations running from salubrious San Diego to Monterey, California, a long way from the dismal Oregon coast that had enveloped and perhaps overborne Lewis three decades earlier. Astonishingly to our contemporary sentiment, when Dana's last three-month tour of these coastal ports concluded he felt he had "just sprung from an iron trap."[17]

Four and a half months later Dana was, per Lewis, home in the bosom of his friends and family. The concluding paragraphs of his original narrative provide further insight into the long-distance traveler's nostalgia for home, thus also helping us to understand the emotional vortex that snared Lewis and contributed to his failure to produce a published account. Dana started by relating the experience of "a sailor whose first voyage was one of five years upon the Northwest Coast." When this seaman

> found himself homeward bound, such was the excitement of his feelings that, during the whole passage, he could talk and think of nothing else but his arrival, and how and when he should jump from the vessel and take his way directly home. Yet, when the vessel was made fast to the wharf and the crew dismissed, he seemed suddenly to lose all feeling about the matter. He told me he went below and changed his dress; took some water from the scuttle butt and washed himself leisurely; overhauled his chest, and put his clothes all in order; took his pipe from its place, filled it, and, sitting down upon his chest, smoked it slowly for the last time. Here he looked round upon the forecastle in which he had spent so many years, and being alone and his shipmates scattered, began to feel actually unhappy. Home became almost a dream; and it was not until his brother (who had heard of the ship's arrival) came down into the forecastle and told him of things at home, and who were waiting there to see him, that he could realize where he was, and feel interest enough to put him in motion toward that place for which he had longed, and of which he had dreamed, for years.[18]

The seaman's malaise was conveyed as a long prologue to Dana's own experience with, and reflections about, this psychological phenomenon. He wrote: "There is probably so much of excitement in prolonged expectation that the quiet realizing of it produces momentary stagnation of feeling as well as of effort. It was a good deal so with me." Dana related that "coming up the harbor, and old scenes breaking upon the view, produced a mental as well as bodily activity, from which the change to a perfect stillness, when both expectation and necessity of labor failed, left a calmness, almost an indifference, from which I must be roused by some new excitement." Here we have a story, in two parts, strongly suggestive of the emotional state Lewis found himself in at the conclusion of his voyage. Dana, like his sailor friend, was finally able to wake "mind and body," but for some travelers—think Lewis—the "momentary stagnation" became permanent.[19]

Having discussed Cook earlier in this chapter, it is worth mentioning in conclusion that the great navigator himself returned to the work of discovery almost immediately after his first two expeditions concluded. With the support of the Admiralty's editors, engravers, and publicists (an infrastructure that Jefferson would have been well advised to provide Lewis), all complementing the many able associates he also had aboard ship, the official accounts of his first two voyages were published two years after their conclusion. (The third was published posthumously, four years after that expedition ended.) But it also seems clear in retrospect that the reason why Cook undertook these expeditions in such quick succession is that he had become accustomed to living at the edge of the world. He thrived there, and long-distance voyaging, notwithstanding the risks and stresses inherent in such enterprises, brought him his greatest satisfaction. It is conceivable, therefore, that aside from editorial support what Lewis most needed upon his return was not a governor's chair but another expedition to lead.

——————— NOTES ———————

1. Gary E. Moulton, ed., *The Journals of the Lewis & Clark Expedition* (Lincoln: University of Nebraska Press, 1983–2001), 6: 151–52.
2. Elliott Coues, *History of the Expedition under the Command of Lewis and Clark*, reprint ed. (New York: Dover, 1965), 2: 742.
3. John C. Beaglehole, ed., *The* Endeavour *Journal of Joseph Banks, 1768–1771* (Sydney: Angus and Robertson, 1962), 2: 145.
4. Beaglehole, Endeavour *Journal*, 1: 45.
5. George Forster, *A Voyage Round the World*, Nicholas Thomas and Oliver Berghof, eds. (Honolulu: University of Hawaii Press, 2000), 1: 292.
6. John C. Beaglehole, ed. *The Journals of Captain James Cook on His Voyages of Discovery* (London: Cambridge University Press, 1955–67), 2: 322.
7. Beaglehole, *Journals*, 2: 325; Forster, *Voyage*, 1: 295.

8. Frank McLynn, *Captain Cook: Master of the Seas* (New Haven, CT: Yale University Press, 2011), 398. Although McLynn's synopsis represents the orthodox understanding that Cook was ill-advised to undertake a third voyage and paid the price with his own life, I have offered a contrarian view of the great navigator's fitness to serve and thoroughness of execution during the third voyage in *Captain Cook Rediscovered: Voyaging in the Icy Latitudes* (Vancouver: University of British Columbia Press, 2020).

9. To his daughter Martha, Jefferson wrote, from Aix-en-Provence, on May 28, 1787, "of all the cankers of human happiness, none corrodes it with so silent, yet so baneful a tooth, as indolence. body & mind both unemployed, our being becomes a burthen, & every object about us loathsome, even the dearest. idleness begets ennui, ennui the hypochondria, & that a diseased body. no laborious person was ever yet hysterical. exercise & application produce order in our affairs, health of body, chearfulness of mind, & these make us precious to our friends. it is while we are young that the habit of industry is formed, if not then, it never is afterwards." Thomas Jefferson to Martha Jefferson Randolph, March 28, 1787, "Jefferson Quotes and Family Letters," Thomas Jefferson Monticello, http://tjrs.monticello.org/letter/1679, accessed March 26, 2020. It is worthy of remark that the themes raised by Jefferson in this letter (youth, indolence, industriousness) are a strong evocation of James Thomson's "The Castle of Indolence," discussed in chapter 3.

10. David L. Nicandri, *River of Promise: Lewis and Clark on the Columbia* (Bismarck, ND: Dakota Institute Press, 2009), 247–66.

11. Moulton, *Journals*, 8: 370–71. Drouillard's initial stewardship of Lewis's letter to Jefferson was mirrored by William Clark's entrusting to Sergeant Patrick Gass correspondence to his brother Jonathan Clark that was intended to get news of the expedition into print. See James J. Holmberg, "Getting Out the Word," *We Proceeded On* 27: 3 (August 2001): 12–17.

12. Donald Jackson, ed., *Letters of the Lewis and Clark Expedition with Related Documents: 1783–1854*, 2nd ed. (Urbana: University of Illinois Press, 1978), 1: 324.

13. Ibid., 2: 442–45.

14. Ibid., 2: 458.

15. Moulton, *Journals*, 4: 285.

16. Richard Henry Dana Jr. *Two Years Before the Mast*, reprint ed. (New York: Signet Classics, 2009), 231–32.

17. Ibid., 234–36, 250.

18. Ibid., 335–36.

19. Ibid., 336.

CHAPTER 8

LEWIS'S "DEAR FRIEND" MAHLON DICKERSON AND THE FATE OF EARLY NINETEENTH-CENTURY AMERICAN EXPLORATION

A single figure bridges three of the greatest explorers in American history, yet in the literature of each they are unconnected one from the others. The only historian to even hint at the intersection of Meriwether Lewis, Charles Wilkes, and John C. Frémont was the ever astute Donald Jackson. In his *Letters of the Lewis and Clark Expedition*, Jackson briefly noted that Mahlon Dickerson "touched the lives of three notable American explorers."[1] Dickerson's connection to Lewis was intensely personal whereas in regard to Wilkes's voyage he played a central policy role. His relationship with Frémont was the most oblique of the three associations, but nonetheless foundational. Spanning nearly forty years, Dickerson's serial engagement with what must be considered the holy trinity of nineteenth-century American explorers is a story long in need of a fuller telling.

New Jersey native Dickerson (1770–1853) graduated from Princeton in 1789 and was admitted to that state's bar in 1793. A committed nationalist, he joined the New Jersey militia that helped suppress the Whiskey Rebellion in 1794. Three years later he moved to Philadelphia, where he practiced law until 1810. A life-long bachelor, he referred to Lewis as "the most sincere friend I ever had." (The feeling was mutual. In the one letter we have from Lewis to Dickerson he referred to him as a "dear friend.") In 1811 Dickerson returned to New Jersey, where his career in politics soared. That same year he was elected to the state general assembly and to a judgeship two years later. He was elected governor of New Jersey in

1815, followed by sixteen years as a U.S. senator. Dickerson reentered the discovery nexus in 1834 when Andrew Jackson appointed him secretary of the navy, then as now a cabinet position.[2]

In some important aspects the life of Lewis (1774–1809), brief as it was, mirrored Dickerson's. Only four years younger than Dickerson, Lewis was also an American nationalist and, as the factional tendencies of the early republic matured, an avowed Jeffersonian Republican. Lewis served in the frontier army, where he first met William Clark, and with these solid political credentials Thomas Jefferson tabbed Lewis, a fellow Virginian, as his personal secretary after his election as president in 1800. (Technically, because of the electoral vote tie with Aaron Burr, the House of Representatives did not elect Jefferson to the presidency until February 1801.) The historiography of Lewis and Clark trumpets the former's habitation in the Presidential Mansion (the term "White House" did not become common until after the War of 1812, a function of a coat of paint that was applied to its exterior after the British tried to burn it). Thus, to use modern parlance, Lewis had plenty of "quality time" with the great American polymath. But, as Donald Jackson pointed out, his existence on Pennsylvania Avenue "performing menial tasks" became "a monotonous routine." Lewis's only deviation from the mundane occurred during his occasional trips to Monticello (near his own home) in Charlottesville and what turned out to be a memorable trip to Philadelphia in 1802 where he spent leisure time with a new friend and fellow Republican partisan—Dickerson.[3]

Lewis and Dickerson first met at Jefferson's White House dinner table on April 19, 1802. Dickerson was there to discuss Republican Party issues in New Jersey and Pennsylvania. We do not know what Jefferson gleaned from that conversation, but Lewis discovered a kindred spirit. When Congress adjourned for the year in early May (as was customary in that era), the president headed home to enjoy a month's vacation. Lewis took leave as well, though his destination was Philadelphia, presumably at the invitation of Dickerson. Unlike his subsequent sojourns to the City of Brotherly Love in 1803 and 1807, bracketing his expedition to the Pacific Northwest, Lewis's visit in the spring of 1802 was purely recreational. There was no political or governmental work requiring Lewis's presence there but the trip, intentionally or not, proved productive for Dickerson because soon thereafter Jefferson made him the federal bankruptcy magistrate for Philadelphia.[4]

Lewis spent twelve days (May 13–24, 1802) in Philadelphia and the neighboring countryside, many of which were spent, in whole or in part, with Dickerson. We know this because Donald Jackson's *Letters*, a vital documentary record for the study of Lewis and Clark, went to a second edition primarily because of his discovery of Dickerson's diary. Therein we find Dickerson reporting that he spent the evening of May 13 at the home of Thomas McKean (Pennsylvania governor and former member of the Continental Congress and signer of the Declaration of Independence) in the company of "Capt. Meriwether Lewis—private secretary to the President." The next night the two young gentlemen went to a magic and ventriloquism show. On May 18 they sat for silhouetted portraits before Charles Saint-Memin. Foreshadowing their more uproarious gallivanting in 1803 and 1807, Dickerson stated the evening of May 19 was spent "at Madmoiselle Fries with Capt. L." After a workmanlike inspection of the city's waterworks, the two rode out to the home of Senator George Logan—physician, founding member of the American Philosophical Society (APS), and a friend of Jefferson—for dinner. Lewis was probably a member of the "large" company of people who on May 23 joined Dickerson in dining at the home of Alexander James Dallas, the U.S. attorney for eastern Pennsylvania and later secretary of the treasury under James Madison. The next day they rode over to Wilmington, Delaware, to visit John Dickinson, a revolutionary-era theorist and pamphleteer.[5]

After securing his commission to lead the expedition for Northwestern discovery, Lewis returned to Philadelphia in 1803 where he studied with the luminaries of the APS so as to become better versed in Enlightenment-era science. There Lewis spent his days reading or talking to Benjamin Smith Barton, Benjamin Rush, Robert Patterson, and Caspar Wistar (and Andrew Ellicott in nearby Lancaster), but his frequent companion in the evening was his old pal Dickerson. The two dined together or with other dignitaries seven times in a May fortnight including, one time, "avec Miss Patterson & Miss Nicholas." But this was a business trip for Lewis, not a vacation as before, and his training took priority. He spent most of June studying and later that summer his expedition began in earnest.[6]

After returning to Washington, DC, at the conclusion of their voyage to the Pacific Northwest, both Lewis and Clark received new appointments. The former became governor of the new Louisiana Territory (in 1807 constituted as that part of the Louisiana Purchase north of the thirty-third parallel; south of that became for a time the Territory of Orleans); the latter was appointed the chief Indian agent and brigadier general of the territorial militia. Characteristically, the continually diligent Clark left the capital promptly for St. Louis in March 1807, stopping in Fincastle, Virginia, to become engaged to Julia Hancock. It took Lewis more than a year longer to reach St. Louis and assume his post, arguably a more important one than Clark's. Ostensibly Lewis was focused on preparing his account of the Pacific expedition and otherwise planning for its publication. Indeed, because he had more formal education and correspondingly far better writing skills, Lewis was solely responsible for authoring the official narrative, an arrangement in the same mode as Captain Cook for the British Admiralty in the 1770s and George Vancouver, who worked on his literally unto his death in 1798.

In practice, however, Lewis did relatively little along these lines. After arriving in Philadelphia, the young nation's intellectual capital, in mid-April 1807, he started making arrangements with a publisher and for the disposition of the natural history specimens collected during the expedition. Lewis does not appear in Dickerson's diary until June 7, no doubt after finishing the prospectus for his book, an announcement published on June 16. However, unlike 1802 and 1803, this time Dickerson's diary, relative to his association with Lewis, was "archly discrete," to use the characterization of Thomas C. Danisi and John C. Jackson. During the balance of June until Lewis departed Philadelphia in late July, Dickerson's diary emphasized long walks late into the night around the city's parks and public squares with Lewis and, as Danisi and Jackson phrase it, the attention they paid "to the ladies they found excuses to visit, and sometimes revisit." It seems Lewis was attempting to replicate Clark's matrimonial strategy of finding a wife before heading to the frontier. Dickerson and Lewis dined with political figures far less often in 1807 than they did earlier in the decade, filling their time with more jocular if not rowdy activities. Attending meetings of the APS or visiting the Peale Museum and sitting for a portrait could not possibly be considered unbecoming, nor attending the rehearsal and then the public performance of a patriotic play ("The Glory of Columbia, Her Yeomanry"). But as spring turned to early summer the more representative and perhaps problematic entries in Dickerson's diary refer to such outings as "eating and drinking and shooting at the trees." Tellingly, Dickerson reports keeping himself "very sober" on July 4, a big day of celebration for the young nation, though the comment may have been tongue-in-cheek, implying an opposite state of deportment.[7]

More ominously, on July 13 Dickerson discretely recorded "my Friend Capt. L in trouble." Clay Jenkinson states that this line "could mean almost anything." Donald Jackson concluded the turn of phrase was "probably connected with the attention he was lavishing on Philadelphia women." Jenkinson, more particularly, suggests that something had gone awry in Lewis's courtship of Ann Randolph, Jefferson's granddaughter. More apologetically, Danisi and Jackson point out that Dickerson was some-how simply being a good friend but, as Jenkinson avers, this notation "was unlikely to have signified a positive development in Lewis's life."[8]

Along that line, less than a week later, after leaving a meeting of the APS, Dickerson was on another walkabout "with Capt. Lewis" when they witnessed a "fracas" which resulted in a party being "cut under the eye." This and similar excursions the preceding week resemble what today would be called a pub crawl, with somewhat predictable consequences. Stephen E. Ambrose suggested that the stop at this particular watering hole "certainly sounds like a barroom brawl." In any event, three days later Dickerson portentously recorded that he saw Lewis "perhaps for the last time." This proved true, notwithstanding written correspondence in the interim. Sometime later, Dickerson underscored this diary text and offered as an addendum, "saw him no more."[9]

Lewis's time in Philadelphia, with Dickerson or otherwise, was only a portion of what Jenkinson calls his "lost year," which ran from March 1807 to March 1808. Lewis managed to publish his own prospectus and tried to suppress Sgt. Patrick Gass's unauthorized account, but he seemingly made no progress on the actual manuscript. From this sequence Jenkinson concludes: "One of two things is true. Either Lewis actually believed that he would finish his [narrative] in the next nine months, or he was merely attempting to buy time with the public by proposing a publication date that he knew he could not meet, but that he hoped would discourage people from buying Gass's book." In any event, rather than grinding out his book Lewis advanced neither his literary objective nor his incipient polit-ical career that beckoned in St. Louis. Yes, he had identified a publisher and potential illustrators but otherwise, Jenkinson notes, "he seems to have spent his time drinking and carousing with his friend Mahlon Dicker-son…and trying to find a suitable wife."[10]

The only letter we have in Lewis's hand from his spring and summer in Philadelphia was sent to President Jefferson on June 27, 1807. This mis-sive, transported to the capital by no less a figure than Secretary of War Henry Dearborn, covered a package containing a ring and "Majr. Ran-dolph's watch." This was likely a reference to Jefferson's son-in-law Thomas

Randolph Jr., because Randolph Sr., who held the rank of colonel in the Virginia militia, died in 1793. Lewis told his mentor and patron "the ring has been reset with the addition of four new brilliants," small stones set around a larger diamond in order to make it shine brighter. The ring's style is strongly suggestive of being a woman's, perhaps even the late Mrs. Jefferson's wedding ring. "Knowing it to be a family piece," Lewis wrote, "I directed the workman to reset it in the same stile it formerly was, but regardless of the charge he took the liberty of consulting his own taste on the subject and has made it such as I fear will not prove pleasing to you."[11]

By this point in time, nine months had passed since the end of the Pacific expedition without Lewis having prepared the manuscript which Jefferson awaited more than anyone. Now he had bungled the repair of the president's heirloom. Fortunately, "the watch of Mrs. Randolph," Jefferson's daughter Martha, was "in readiness," later to be carried to Washington by Secretary of State Albert Gallatin when he passed through Philadelphia on his way from New York City to Washington. A third watch, the president's, "is not yet repared." Lewis put it in the jeweler's possession "immediately on my arrival at this place; my visits to him on that subject," Lewis continued, "have not been unfrequent since, and he has after many apologies… promised me that she shall be ready in the course of a few days." These circumstances are perhaps the most benign explanation of Dickerson's diary entry suggesting his friend Lewis was "in trouble."[12]

Lewis's only known letter to Dickerson was written from his home in Albemarle County, Virginia, on November 3, 1807. It had been over a year since the end of the expedition and only now was he planning to return to St. Louis to assume his governorship. The nominal purpose of this missive was to convey John Marks, his half brother, to Dickerson's "friendly care" while young Marks attended school in Philadelphia. Lewis stated he "enjoined him to call on you frequently, as for all those little matters of advice, admonition, &c., for which he would have called on me had I been personally present."[13]

Donald Jackson defended the inclusion of this letter in his compendium that was otherwise "devoted primarily to the expedition…because the manuscript provides a rare view of Lewis's enigmatic personal life." And indeed, historians have found Lewis's discursive enhancements in this missive ripe for interpretation because its contents quickly transition from the "business" of his relative's care to "the *girls*" back in Philadelphia, a phrase he used twice. The identity of Lewis's love interests now matters little, other than to specify they were female. This is important to note as it seemingly belies recent speculation that Lewis had a "minority sexual orientation" in the form of an "intimate partnership" with Clark. The author of that hypothesis, William Benemann, professes that he relies on a "tenuous chain of supposition" to support the existence of this purported "passionate attachment" and admits "we may never know whether this intimacy included a physical component." That said, few could argue with Benemann when he states "their relationship is central to their story" and that Lewis was "emotionally attached to William Clark."[14] Certainly his partner's marriage to Hancock complicated Lewis's problematic circumstances once he assumed office in St. Louis because Mrs. Clark, in effect, kicked him out of her household.

There is a certain poignancy to Lewis's declaration to Dickerson that he was *"a perfect widower with rispect to love."* Most commentators focus on Lewis's expressed sense of "restlessness" and "inquietude," usually overlooking an aspect of the letter that established a sense of mutuality with Dickerson. Lewis referred to a loss of "that certain indiscribable something common to old bachelors," not *an* old bachelor. Lewis follows with a nod toward "that *void in our hearts*, which might, or ought to be better filled." That void, we may assume, was also felt by Dickerson and expressed to Lewis on their nighttime walks around Philadelphia. This explains the deep bond of understanding that framed their friendship and sense of shared loss. Speaking for himself, Lewis stated, "I never felt less like a heroe than at the present moment." He was, nonetheless, determined *"to get a wife."*[15]

Lewis concluded his letter to Dickerson by asking for news "about *the girls*," those "bewitching gipsies," especially "Miss E_____ B____y." The ellipses resemble modern teenage banter. Indeed, Jenkinson asserts this text, written by a thirty-three-year-old man, "is the stuff of arrested adolescence." Tragically, Lewis was about to head west again without having leveraged his fame as an explorer "into a successful sexual and romantic relationship with a woman," Jenkinson adds. Since the Lewis story ends in suicide, Jenkinson deems this a "cry of anguish by a man whose life was seriously off track." Without question, Lewis's letter to Dickerson is one the most revealing texts he ever wrote.[16]

The principal theme of the Dickerson letter was not a one-off. Nearly nine months later, on July 25, 1808, Lewis, now ensconced in St. Louis and doing his best to survive the political turmoil he was caught up in there, wrote a similar letter to another old friend from the army, William Preston in Kentucky. Preston was Clark's brother-in-law; that is to say, they married the Hancock sisters. Lewis complained about "how wretchedly you married men arrange the subjects of which you treat." Lewis was driving at the fact that instead of getting to the point of his letter up front, Preston had sequestered to its end news about the marriage the month before of one Letitia Breckinridge, in whom Lewis formerly had a romantic interest. "You have gained that which I have yet to obtain, *a wife*,"[17] Lewis stated with resignation, emphasizing the last two words in his text, just as he had in his letter to Dickerson the previous fall.

A little more than a year later, Lewis was dead by his own hand. It is generally conceded that he shot himself in the early morning hours of October 11, 1809, at Grinder's Stand on the Natchez Trace in Tennessee. One of the more sensational aspects of the death tableau was the report that Lewis had slashed himself with razors as well. Dickerson first read a news account about Lewis's demise on October 22. That night, he edited his otherwise nondescript diary entry for the tenth by adding "poor Meriwether Lewis killd. himself this night." For the October 22 entry, he inscribed: "read the horrible account of Capt. Meriwether Lewis's death on the night of the 10th Oct. I think he was the most sincere friend I ever had."[18]

Danisi found enclosed in Dickerson's papers a faded clipping from the *Democratic Press* (Philadelphia) dated November 13, 1809. This memento of Lewis's life contained the gory details of Lewis's gruesome death scene, including that he appeared to have shot himself either before or after cutting the arteries on his arms and legs. The writer of this ersatz obituary stated this "intelligence" was "confirmed by a gentleman at present in this place." Dickerson could well have been this informant, though any one of the several luminaries in the Philadelphia scientific establishment that had tutored Lewis are just as likely. (Then again, the story about Lewis may have been a reprint of the original published reports detailing Lewis's death in the Nashville press.) In any event, the editorialist puzzled over "the circumstances which led to this unhappy event." The best this writer could ascertain was that "Governor Lewis drew bills to a considerable amount on the government of the United States, for which there had been no specific appropriations and which came back protested."[19]

Historians accept this bureaucratic shamble as relevant context but suicide seems disproportionate to the purported misfeasance. Observers as early and close to Lewis as Jefferson alluded to a pattern of melancholy in the explorer's outlook on life. More particularly, the president seems to have been alluding to Lewis's somewhat dissolute ways, as indeed his carousing with Dickerson exemplifies, when he wrote of "the habit into which [Lewis] had fallen & the painfull reflections that would necessarily produce in a mind like his." Lewis himself had once said as much. In his exploratory journal for August 18, 1805, the night of his thirty-first birthday, he wrote of the "regret" he felt over "the many hours I have spent in indolence" and wished some days in his past had been more "judiciously expended."[20] We must also allow for the possibility that the tragic end of Lewis's career also influenced the way Dickerson later viewed explorers and their work.

With Lewis's suicide, Dickerson virtually disappears from the pages of Lewis and Clark historiography. One of the few mentions in the literature is Ambrose's vague reference to Dickerson as "a politician who later became governor of New Jersey and then a Cabinet officer."[21] But within the context of the history of American exploration it was a very important cabinet position because in 1834 Andrew Jackson appointed him secretary of the navy. In that office he played a vital role relative to the launching of the United States Exploring Expedition.

This venture was commanded by Charles Wilkes and for that reason it is more commonly known as the Wilkes expedition. His voyage (1838–42), modeled after the great Enlightenment voyages of Cook, La Pérouse, and Malaspina, consisted of a multiship flotilla and a large roster of scientists. It was the largest and best-known voyage of discovery in American history until Robert Peary's attempts to reach the North Pole in the late nineteenth and early twentieth centuries. More to the point of our focus, Wilkes conducted the first extensive exploration of the Pacific Northwest since Lewis and Clark. Indeed, his Jacksonian-era expedition was more consequential than the Jeffersonian effort in establishing American sovereignty over a portion of the Oregon Country. Like Lewis and Clark, Wilkes explored the lower Columbia River (one of his ships sank on the bar) and elements of his command ventured all the way to the Nez Perce homelands, but that treaded over old ground. Wilkes's personal survey of the numerous deep-water harbors of Puget Sound (commencing thus Commencement Bay adjoining modern Tacoma, just above The Narrows that led to what Vancouver defined as "Puget's Sound") was a revelation. In the wake of Wilkes's voyage, some American policy makers blustered about fighting Great Britain for terrain extending to 54°40' N, but

Alonzo Chappel, Portrait of Charles Wilkes. An engraving based upon a portrait of Wilkes after he was promoted to rear admiral during the Civil War. Courtesy of the Washington State Historical Society. WSHS 2015.29.9.

that was a tactic intended to create negotiating room for splitting the difference at the forty-ninth parallel that would secure the inland sea accessed by the Strait of Juan de Fuca. That basin, post-Wilkes, was the Oregon Country's real prize.

Dickerson, then, had a strong connection to the first two major scientific exploring expeditions sent to the Pacific Northwest. Furthermore, as much as the lore surrounding Lewis and Clark is silent on Dickerson's later connection to the work of discovery, so too are Wilkes scholars oblivious to Dickerson's friendship with Lewis. More particularly, little consideration has been lent to whether Dickerson's sometimes feckless management of the U.S. Exploring Expedition was somehow influenced by the problematic fate of Lewis.

During the Revolutionary War, the American government had a military arm that went by the title of the Continental Navy (derived from the Continental Congress). At war's end, this navy was disbanded, but under George Washington the U.S. Navy was instituted in 1794 in the wake of threats to the young nation's foreign shipping. Until Wilkes, the American navy's two most notable theaters of war were on Mediterranean waters against the Barbary pirates during the Jefferson administration and on the Great Lakes and Lake Champlain during the War of 1812. For the first three decades of the nineteenth century, the work of American discovery was monopolized by the U.S. Army. That began to change in 1825 when John Quincy Adams became president. He was the first commander in chief since Jefferson to hold an expansive interest in science and other learned endeavors. Adams advocated for a national university (which never eventuated) and a naval observatory (which did in 1842, after he left office), but more central to our interest was his advocacy for a voyage to the Pacific Northwest to follow up on Lewis and Clark's pioneering effort. His initiative was stillborn in the era of emergent Jacksonian continentalism, an expansionist philosophy recognized in the ensuing generation as "manifest destiny."

As so often happened in the centuries-long comprehension of North American and polar geography, external and purely hypothetical speculation by armchair geographers changed the course of exploration history. For example, James Cook launched his third and final voyage toward the North Pole in response to Daines Barrington's pamphlet (1775) that argued it was possible to sail from the Pacific to the Atlantic through a seasonally ice-free Arctic Ocean, if not over the North Pole itself. Vancouver was dispatched, in part, to the Northwest Coast a decade and half later to test Alexander Dalrymple's published theory (1789) that the Pacific slope of North America contained a deep opening into the continental interior that was analogous to the indent of Hudson Bay off the Atlantic. By the 1820s John Cleves Symmes Jr. re-propagated Barrington's idea (which Cook thought he had permanently discredited) that above the Arctic ice edge lay a mild climate and open water. Even more fantastically, Symmes theorized that from the poles it was possible to transect the earth's mantle and gain access to the planet's subterranean interior.

Symmes's "Holes in the Poles" hypothesis (also commonly known as the Hollow Earth theory) was the apex of two centuries' worth of credulous geographic speculation about the Arctic. Nevertheless, it caught the attention of Jeremiah N. Reynolds, an Ohio newspaperman. Over several years' time Reynolds mobilized the seafaring trade and scientific societies of the eastern seaboard and in 1828 he secured an appointment as special agent to the navy charged with executing an exploring expedition. One aspect of his charge was the identification of candidates to fill out the scientific complement. This process identified Wilkes, the eventual commander a decade later, as a potential astronomer. But shifting political tides killed Reynolds's momentum. Later that year Adams lost the presidency to Andrew Jackson, who as a candidate campaigned as an advocate for a continental outlook, which only added to the headwinds against the expedition already blowing from a skeptical Congress.

The Symmes/Reynolds/Pacific–Polar expedition languished for the next seven years but, in an unexpected turnabout, over the course of his presidency Jackson gradually discerned what a navy could do to advance national aims. Collaterally he developed an interest in exploration. The tide began to turn in 1831. In an action resembling Jefferson's sudden affinity for naval intervention abroad to defend the nation's honor, Jackson dispatched the frigate *Potomac* to the East Indies to punish pirates who had been raiding American merchantmen near Sumatra. Reynolds happened to be an adjutant to the captain of that ship. His stirring account (published in 1834) assuaged the nation's pride while Jackson harvested the political reward. Flush with naval success, in his annual message to Congress on December 1 of that same year the peppery Jackson bluntly signaled an inclination to take forceful action against France, which was refusing to pay 25 million francs in claims that had grown out of the seizure of American ships dating to the Napoleonic era. The United States made good on the threat with vigorous naval preparations in 1835, which prompted France to send a squadron to its colonies in the West Indies for defensive purposes. War was averted in early 1836 through British mediation, although the United States was rewarded with the French payment of debt.

There were also internal political forces at play in Jackson's newfound interest in the navy. During the South Carolina secession threat of 1831–32, Jackson stationed much of the national fleet off Charleston harbor, forcing John C. Calhoun to stand down over tariffs. This made Jackson temporarily popular in maritime-oriented New England. Indeed, when the *Constitution* was restored in 1833, the naval commodore in Boston commissioned a figurehead of Jackson for the prow of "Old Ironsides," America's most storied vessel. Jackson's momentary acceptance in New England faded in the aftermath of the Bank of the United States controversy, most graphically signified by someone cutting the head off the sculpture. The offender was never apprehended, and a new figurehead was commissioned, but the mutilated pate of the original was retrieved through back-channel sources and presented to the secretary of the navy, Dickerson. It was still in his possession when his estate was settled in 1854.

Sensing Jackson's growing enthusiasm for nautical affairs and naval power, Reynolds accelerated his advocacy for an exploring expedition, including an address to Congress in the spring of 1836, Jackson's last full year as president. In his speech, Reynolds pitched a scientific voyage to the Pacific and Antarctic seas with a scope that included studies of magnetism, volcanism, natural history, and other fields of interest. Jackson intervened personally, hoping to see Congress authorize the venture before he left office by playing a central role overcoming the resistance of southern

Democrats, his customary allies. Like Jackson himself before he became president, this caucus was normally only interested in pressing a continental expansionist agenda, chiefly to secure more lands for growing cotton. Jackson's motivation was not principally a response to scientific concerns (fanciful or otherwise) but rather the demands of maritime interests who were eager to find new whaling and sealing grounds in the southern Atlantic and Pacific. As early as 1828 the citizens of Nantucket, Rhode Island, sent a memorial to Washington, pleading for a government-sponsored expedition to search for "new islands, and reefs."[22]

Jackson was able to push Congress into funding what was now construed as a South Seas expedition by linking the venture to the prospects of national expansion. Unlike Texas and the balance of the Louisiana Purchase to the limits of the Continental Divide, the Oregon Country was a great leap to the far western edge of the continent. An exploring expedition to the Pacific Northwest could expedite the country's continental ambitions that might otherwise languish because of intervening distances and obstacles, human and natural. That is, a naval voyage to the Pacific could serve as an end run around potentially hostile Indian tribes and inhospitable mountain ranges. Jackson's advocacy was ironically consistent with Jefferson's support of the Lewis and Clark Expedition in that two strict constructionists abandoned their normative constitutional principles to forward the pursuit of discovery.

Here, Dickerson, now sixty-six years old, reenters our story. Still a bachelor, wealthy, and a member of the APS (with a personal interest in botany), he was a true Jeffersonian in the age of Jackson with his love of gardening and small government. But unlike Jefferson or Jackson, Dickerson was fundamentally incapable of transcending his ideological limits. Just when Jackson had come around to the idea of engaging in maritime expansion, Dickerson remained committed to a small navy. Though dedicated to science, he fended off all attempts to create a naval academy, and when Congress finally authorized the United States Exploring Expedition, Dickerson advised Jackson to cancel it—advice the latter rejected. Filling a leadership vacuum, Jeremiah N. Reynolds began to pull a scientific team together and scouted ships to constitute the small squadron. This effort, Nathaniel Philbrick writes, required "an immense amount of planning and cooperation on the part of the U.S. Navy," but unfortunately, "the man who should have been the Expedition's most zealous proponent [Dickerson] was, in fact, its principal detractor, applying what little reserves of energy he possessed in deploying strategies to delay its departure."[23]

One additional reason for Jackson's enthusiasm for the naval expedition lay in the fact that Thomas ap Catesby Jones [*sic*], an old comrade from the Battle of New Orleans, was in line to command it. Because of that affinity, Jackson told Dickerson that Jones was to have final approval of all officers serving under him. More specifically, the president insisted that naval publicist Reynolds had to be included on Jones's staff. In Philbrick's estimation, "Dickerson would do his best to subvert" Jackson's directives. Reynolds was the key to this denouement because he happened to be a good friend of one of Dickerson's old political foes from New Jersey and he "did everything in his power to exclude him."[24]

While Dickerson and Jones bickered over the junior officers during the summer of 1836, the former sent the eventual commander, Wilkes, to England to secure copies of the latest charts from British and Russian exploration of the Southern Ocean plus navigational instruments and training in their use. After Cook and Vancouver failed to find successive versions of the Northwest Passage, European and American nautical interest turned to the Southern Hemisphere, focusing on the location of whaling and sealing grounds especially. Dispatching Wilkes to London, the international center of geographic and navigational science, mirrored Jefferson's decision to send Lewis to Philadelphia in 1803. Wilkes returned to the United States in January 1837 with the latest maps and forty precious English chronometers to help the American expedition establish longitude during its Cook-like circumnavigation of the globe. By way of this maneuver Dickerson was able to delay the launch of the expedition into the administration of Martin Van Buren, who became president in March.

Dickerson survived to the new cabinet, but before leaving office Jackson told him to settle on the complement of men for the several ships. That did not happen for months, but Dickerson was not the only influence upon that turn of events. Historian William H. Goetzmann explains: "Few officers of rank wanted anything to do with shepherding a boatload of effete 'scientifics' around the world."[25] This attitude actually mirrored Captain Cook's demeanor in advance of his final expedition as he too, after wrangling with civilian naturalists on his second voyage, wanted a cleaner line of shipboard command and comity.

A contentious dynamic was endemic to the early planning of the expedition. Whereas Dickerson squabbled with Jones, he also quarreled with Wilkes who, as a navy man, refused to sail as the voyage's astronomer if he had to report to a civilian. At the same time, Dickerson was under a barrage of applications from American scientists who wanted to go on the voyage. (From the vantage of 1836 it is easy to see in retrospect the appeal of Jefferson's selection of Lewis as a commander but training him to be the lead naturalist as well.) Dickerson, buffeted by intermittent naval indifference to a project that complemented his own apathy, began to ignore the expedition and, in Goetzmann's phrasing, "spent most of his time at his favorite hobby, horticulture, hoping that the whole expedition project would simply die of neglect."[26]

Reynolds went public with his and others' grievances against Dickerson in June 1837. The infighting and delay not only cost the expedition the services of Nathaniel Hawthorne, but also a financial panic hit with full force, thereby casting further doubt on the practicability of launching the voyage. Frustrated by personal and professional differences, postponements, and deteriorating health, Jones resigned his command in November. President Van Buren now realized that Dickerson was neither willing nor able to get the expedition underway and in an unprecedented move put the head of another cabinet agency, Secretary of War Joel Poinsett, in charge of finding a new commander. Poinsett held the reputation as a can-do man. A former congressman from South Carolina, he was later minister to Mexico (where he became familiar with a local plant which he brought home and made famous).

With this problematic history, it should have been no surprise that all the navy's senior officers refused the opportunity to succeed Jones. Thus, the position fell to the only officer with a long-standing interest in the mission, Wilkes, a very junior lieutenant on the seniority roster and a man with little actual sailing experience. He was by this point reasonably accomplished as a surveyor/astronomer, in part because of the seasoning Dickerson afforded him by virtue of the trip to England. Poinsett's choice of Wilkes was not a popular decision. Notwithstanding the fact that all the most senior men turned the job down, some congressmen heaped scorn upon a presumed "violation of rank."[27]

Wilkes's defenders tried to posit the Cook analogy—a surveyor/astronomer appointed to lead an expedition with global reach. Cook, however, had successfully led a multiyear charting of Newfoundland's complex coastline, which service he parlayed into his first voyage to the Pacific to observe the transit of Venus in 1769. Thus, Wilkes had nowhere near the practical surveying experience Cook had, nor did he possess any of the navigational and shipboard management skills that made Cook the most productive explorer of his or any time.

Alfred. T. Agate, *Astoria, Columbia River,* in *Narrative of the United States Exploring Expedition,* by Charles Wilkes (Philadelphia: Lea & Blanchard, 1845), 5: 119. An engraving from Wilkes's account of his expedition, from a drawing by Agate. Aside from the mammoth flag of the United States flying above the remnants of Fort Astoria, an early fur trade post established in the wake of the Lewis and Clark Expedition, the scene is noteworthy for its precise delineation of the headlands on the north bank of the river. From left to right, Cape Disappointment, Scarboro Hill/Chinook Point, and Point Ellice (partially obscured by a tree in the foreground). Courtesy of the Washington State Historical Society. WSHS 1943.42.63021.

But Wilkes's appointment did echo the experience of yet another explorer. In order to exercise proper chain of command and squadron discipline, Wilkes expected a promotion to captain. This was reminiscent of Clark who, after responding favorably to Lewis's invitation to join the expedition to the Pacific Northwest, expected follow-through on the promise of a captaincy. Congress did not comply, but Clark soldiered on. As I have written elsewhere, in many ways Clark was more accomplished than Lewis as a leader of men, river navigator, and geographic problem solver.[28]

If Wilkes was no Cook he was not Clark either. He chafed at the idea that he might be outranked by peers from other nations' navies he might encounter in distant harbors. Wilkes believed that he had secured a commitment for a promotion from Dickerson, who as secretary of the navy was still his nominal superior and in a position to help make it happen. But Dickerson saw the voyage essentially as a civil affair, not a naval endeavor.

Poinsett, who was the ultimate decision maker, was averse to compounding the scorn he already faced for appointing Wilkes to begin with. Wilkes told Poinsett that he would never have accepted the mission if he had known the promotion was not to be forthcoming. He professed that a captaincy would "give force to my position and surround me with, as it were, a shield of protection."[29] Insecure in the knowledge that he had less sailing experience than many of his midshipmen, Wilkes frequently over-reacted to slights, real and imagined, resulting in the most fractious of any Enlightenment or post-Enlightenment voyage of discovery.

The course of the Wilkes voyage to Antarctica and the Oregon Country is outside the remit of this essay so only a few summary and topically relevant observations shall be offered here. The United States Exploring Expedition sailed out of Norfolk in 1838, returning in 1842. It was, as Philbrick notes, "the last all-sail naval squadron to circumnavigate the world."[30] His ships covered 87,000 miles and surveyed 280 islands in the Pacific Basin, resulting in ethnological and botanical collections that eventually became the foundation of the Smithsonian Institution. The voyage also made possible the production of 180 charts, including that which detailed 800 miles of Pacific Northwest coastal and inland waters. As noted above, Wilkes's survey of the deep waters of Admiralty Inlet (now commonly known as Puget Sound) convinced policy makers in the nation's capital that it was the treasure of the Oregon Country. This enabled American diplomats to back off from claims on the entire country up to 54°40' N and instead settle on a westward extension of the forty-ninth parallel from the Rocky Mountains to salt water as the dividing line with British territory. Wilkes also modeled Alexander Mackenzie and Lewis by bringing along a Newfoundland dog—"Sydney"—a continuation of the common affectation of explorers during that era.

As for Lewis's "dear friend" Dickerson, he resigned as navy secretary the same year Wilkes finally got underway, but before leaving office he made one more lasting contribution to the history of exploration in the Northwest. Dickerson gave a young Frémont his start in the field of scientific discovery by appointing him as a mathematical instructor at sea in 1833. Frémont later resigned from the navy to join the army's Corps of Topographical Engineers. Notwithstanding the early planning for what became the Wilkes expedition, terrestrial exploration was always going to be the main outlet for the discovery impulse in midcentury America and so Frémont went in that direction. He was the first army explorer to tread a portion of the Lewis and Clark trail west of the Continental Divide. Indeed, Frémont's charts of the

Columbia Basin, once conjoined with his other work in the lands adjoining the lower Missouri River, created a veritable trail guide for land-hungry immigrants who started to pour into the Oregon Country in the 1840s and 1850s. In that way, Frémont helped forge the overland link that bound the Mississippi Valley to the Pacific Northwest, finishing the canvas Jefferson first envisioned a half century earlier.

————————— NOTES —————————

1. Donald Jackson, ed., *Letters of the Lewis and Clark Expedition with Related Documents: 1783– 1854*, 2nd ed. (Urbana: University of Illinois Press, 1978), 2: 677.
2. Charles F. Reed, "Mahlon Dickerson," *Discovering Lewis & Clark* (May 2005), http://www.lewis-clark.org/article/2323, accessed March 28, 2020.
3. Donald C. Jackson, *Thomas Jefferson and the Rocky Mountains: Exploring the West from Monticello* (Norman: University of Oklahoma Press, 2002), 121.
4. Jackson, *Letters*, 2: 678.
5. Ibid., 2: 678–79.
6. Ibid., 2: 679–81.
7. Thomas C. Danisi and John C. Jackson, *Meriwether Lewis* (Amherst, NY: Prometheus Books, 2009), 171; Jackson, *Letters*, 2: 681–83.
8. Jackson, *Letters*, 2; 683; Clay Jenkinson, *The Character of Meriwether Lewis: Explorer in the Wilderness* (Bismarck, ND: Dakota Institute Press, 2011), 330; Danisi and Jackson, *Lewis*, 172.
9. Jackson, *Letters*, 2: 684, 689; Stephen E. Ambrose, *Undaunted Courage: Meriwether Lewis, Thomas Jefferson, and the Opening of the American West* (New York: Simon & Schuster, 1996), 427.
10. Jenkinson, *Character*, 237.
11. Jackson, *Letters*, 2: 418.
12. Ibid.
13. Ibid., 2: 719.
14. Ibid., 2: 720; William Benneman, "'My Friend and Companion': The Intimate Journey of Lewis and Clark," *We Proceeded On* 41: 1 (February 2015): 5, 9–10, 13 and 41: 2 (May 2015): 30.
15. Jackson, *Letters*, 2: 720.
16. Ibid. 2: 270; Jenkinson, *Character*, 331–32.
17. Quoted in Ambrose, *Undaunted Courage*, 439.
18. Jackson, *Letters*, 2: 684.
19. Danisi and Jackson, *Lewis*, 328–29.
20. Jackson, *Letters*, 2: 575; Gary E. Moulton, ed., *The Definitive Journals of the Lewis and Clark Expedition* (Lincoln: University of Nebraska Press), 5: 118.
21. Ambrose, *Undaunted Courage*, 63.
22. Nathaniel Philbrick, *Sea of Glory: America's Voyage of Discovery, The U.S. Exploring Expedition, 1838–1842* (New York: Viking, 2003), 16.
23. Ibid., 31–32.
24. Ibid., 32.
25. William H. Goetzmann, *New Lands, New Men: America and the Second Great Age of Discovery* (New York: Viking, 1986), 271.
26. Ibid.
27. Philbrick, *Sea of Glory*, 48.
28. David L. Nicandri, *River of Promise: Lewis and Clark on the Columbia* (Bismarck, ND: Dakota Institute Press, 2009), 115–40.
29. Philbrick, *Sea of Glory*, 58.
30. Ibid., xix.

WHITHER THE EXPLORATION OF LEWIS AND CLARK:

RECENT TRENDS AND FUTURE DIRECTIONS

The bicentennial of the Lewis and Clark Expedition precipitated a profusion of new publications. Facilitated by Gary E. Moulton's modern edition of the *Journals* (1983–2001), much of this literature was descriptive narration with an orientation toward a localized portion of the trail. These efforts were often quite good at answering the "how" and "what" questions, but not as successful in addressing the "so what?" proposition. Even the most accomplished of these efforts were often derivative in nature, keying off the foundational geographical insights provided by John Logan Allen's *Passage Through the Garden: Lewis and Clark and the Image of the American Northwest* (1975), later reissued and retitled as *Lewis and Clark and the Image of the American Northwest* (1991). Allen's book is still the most influential analysis of the expedition ever written. Among other effects, he popularized the trope of Meriwether Lewis's "disappointment" at the Continental Divide. Notably, his book inspired James P. Ronda's involvement with the Lewis and Clark story.

Prior to 1975, Ronda's area of scholarly focus was a more generalized interest in the history of the early national period, but his exposure to Allen's book (during the course of preparing a book review) stimulated a curiosity about Lewis and Clark. The result was the second most influential book in the recent historiography about the expedition, *Lewis and Clark among the Indians* (1984). Ronda's book was the first one to attempt a look at the expedition as it appeared to Native inhabitants on the riverbank, as opposed to the standard interpretation which was from the vantage of men inside the keelboat or pirogues looking for the next bend in the river.

No book exceeded the popular reach of Stephen E. Ambrose's *Undaunted Courage: Meriwether Lewis, Thomas Jefferson, and the Opening of the American West* (1996), which gave the bicentennial its early momentum. Its success was turbocharged by Ambrose's starring role in the Ken Burns and Dayton Duncan PBS documentary *Lewis and Clark: The Journey of the Corps of Discovery* (1997). This film cemented the Lemhi Disappointment and Bitterroot Mountains starvation myths in popular and scholarly imaginations, and adopted Ambrose's thesis that Lewis was an accomplished but troubled individual, one who perhaps suffered from manic depression. *Undaunted Courage* also transplanted the ethos of Ambrose's *Band of Brothers* (1992), his World War II epic, to the American West with a subtext suggesting that Lewis and Clark enjoyed the greatest friendship of all time.

Burns had been on a trajectory to focus on Duncan's detailed knowledge of the trail landscape, recorded previously in his *Out West: A Journey through Lewis and Clark's America* (1987), combined with Allen's geographic insights and Ronda's desire to tell the story from the Native American perspective. All three are featured in the documentary, but the emergence of *Undaunted Courage* during the production of the film shifted its orientation to an American pageant focusing on a heroic but perturbed Lewis.

The first prominent crack in the modern idealization of the expedition came with Clay S. Jenkinson's *The Character of Meriwether Lewis: 'Completely Metamorphosed' in the American West* (2000). Jenkinson broke ranks from the orthodox interpretation of the expedition by pointing out such things as Lewis's psychological immaturity and his corresponding fondness for striking poses, both in deed and in text. Jenkinson began to suspect that Lewis had engineered the course of the expedition so that the moments of greatest triumph were his alone. Jenkinson's single greatest insight was detecting the artificiality of much of what Lewis wrote going westbound from Fort Mandan to the Nez Perce villages, including his self-absorption in the reveries of being an explorer in previously uncharted lands. In particular, Jenkinson pointed out the studied, one might say artificial, nature of Lewis's journal surrounding the Great Falls of the Missouri and Lemhi Pass sequences.

Jenkinson's breakthrough had been prefigured by Albert Furtwangler's *Acts of Discovery: Visions of America in the Lewis and Clark Journals* (1993), a book that deserves greater attention than it has received. Furtwangler quietly began the interpretive shift away from considering the expedition as an adventure story toward the actual context within which Lewis and Clark's contemporaries understood it. Up to that point most modern histories of the expedition had fostered a visualization of the story as a backward glance toward an American Eden through which readers could envision themselves as latter-day explorers living in a simpler time upon pristine landscapes. Contemporaneously, the relatively few members of the American public forming its cultural elite who actually read Nicholas Biddle's account of the expedition (1814) evaluated it within a comparative literary framework—in juxtaposition to the accounts of James Cook, George Vancouver, and Alexander Mackenzie, for example—not as an outdoor escapade, the mode of interpretation that became so popular with twentieth-century readers.

The first book to fully transcend the micro-universe of Lewis and Clark studies was Thomas P. Slaughter's *Exploring Lewis and Clark: Reflections on Men and Wilderness* (2003). Slaughter did not have the popular sales success of Ambrose, but his treatment captured wide attention among the professoriate. This occurred because of Slaughter's fondness for debunking both the explorers (who were suddenly enjoying national attention as a function of the bicentennial) and those who bothered to study them. Nonetheless, *Exploring Lewis and Clark* is full of interpretive insights, such as documenting the divergences between Lewis's renderings of particular episodes versus Clark's. Seemingly inspired by Jenkinson, Slaughter shows more broadly how Lewis used his journals to create an identity for himself based upon his readings of other explorers' accounts. Slaughter also infused his book with interpretive strategies adapted from postmodern literary studies that had become increasingly popular among academics in their discussions about European-American exploration, particularly those that focused on Captain Cook. This took such forms as his provocative notion that Lewis was already dead (spiritually) when he came home.

Drawing on Jenkinson's opening and Slaughter's incisiveness, I followed with *River of Promise: Lewis and Clark on the Columbia* (2009). Lewis and Clark scholars have long favored the expedition's time on the Missouri principally because of the erudite exposition in Lewis's journal westbound from Fort Mandan to Lemhi Pass. I inverted that focus to concentrate on the portion of their voyage that was central to its actual mission. I also attempted to prove that Lewis's westering journal was not a field diary written each night around the campfire, but was instead a retrospective second-generation reflection probably intended as the first draft of a book he never got around to publishing. Rather than the greatest friendship of all time, Clark was often annoyed by, if not angry about, Lewis's grandstanding attempts to claim all the prized moments of discovery. This included Lewis's expropriation of Clark's insights about the complexity of Rocky Mountain geography, what is sometimes referred to in historiographic terms as "Cameahwait's Geography Lesson."

Jenkinson responded with an enlarged version of *The Character of Meriwether Lewis* (2011), now fixed with a new subtitle: *Explorer in the Wilderness*. Abandoning the interpretive straitjacket of a continuous chronological narrative, Jenkinson took his readers on a discursive ramble through Lewis's life and key episodes from the expedition. His deconstruction of Lewis's demise, in a chapter titled "Why," will serve as the modern standard addressing the one topic that intrigues all scholars of the expedition: what led to Lewis's undoing? In answer to this rhetorical query, Jenkinson cites Thomas Jefferson's failure to provide Lewis a suitable support structure, Lewis's somewhat adolescent attitudes about women, his complicated family relationships, his struggles with writer's block, and physical and mental illnesses, including alcoholism.

Seemingly timed as a rejoinder to Slaughter, Thomas C. Danisi and John C. Jackson published *Meriwether Lewis* in 2009. Adulatory toward its subject in the same fashion as Ambrose's *Undaunted Courage*, their biography uncovered new sources documenting the Lewis story and gave emphasis to the novel theory that the aftereffect of malaria was the principal cause of his unraveling. They thereby provided the perfect synthesis in reply to the problem that has faced students of the expedition since October 1809. Yes, Lewis killed himself, but he did so accidentally in a hazy reaction to the pain he was suffering from a malarial recurrence; thus the act does not deserve the stigmatization that suicide brings. A few years later, Danisi followed with a solo effort, *Uncovering the Truth About Meriwether Lewis* (2012). He again broke new ground in an exposition on Lewis's 1795 court-martial and displayed his trademark assiduousness in finding new documentary material.

By adding in the non-expedition specific bicentennial era scholarship of James Holmberg, Landon Jones, William Foley, and Jay Buckley, William Clark has been brought out from under Lewis's shadow forever. But by giving him a more visible place in the expeditionary story scholars have necessarily shone light on his standing as a slaveholder, including his problematic post-expeditionary treatment of York, and his role in the treaty process that dispossessed so many Missouri Basin tribes. This has undone the prospects for making a hero of Clark, so now we are left with *two* challenging figures at the center of the story.

Where does the study of Lewis and Clark go from here?

To start, the literature of Lewis and Clark would be well served by the application of an interdisciplinary approach to the study of the expedition. Bernard Smith did this for the investigation of Captain Cook in his classics—*European Vision and the South Pacific, 1768–1850* (1960) and *Imagining the Pacific: In the Wake of the Cook Voyages* (1992). Regrettably, just as Smith published the second of these books, the study of Cook was inundated by the intemperance of several postcolonial authors. (This was an ironic turn in literary history because Smith was one of the first writers to introduce the term "postmodern" to scholarly usage, a typology that was later expanded to include the derivative term "postcolonial.") As an Australian scholar, Smith had the singular advantage of recourse to that country's voluminous archive of paintings, sketches, and charts generated by the artists and draftsmen aboard Cook's ships during the passage of three global voyages. In what must be regarded as Jefferson's greatest oversight, no artist was attached to the first great American expedition.

Even though art history is thus precluded as a disciplinary option for the future study of Lewis and Clark, there are still other opportunities. For example, follow-ups to Daniel Botkin's environmental studies (*Our Natural History: The Lessons of Lewis and Clark* [1995] and *Beyond the Stony Mountains: Nature in the American West from Lewis and Clark to Today* [2004]) are long overdue. These could involve localized analyses of such places as the riverscapes of the Great Falls of the Missouri or The Dalles on the Columbia, or discussions of particular species such as birds, fish, or bears. On a grander scale, extensive syntheses of the three great biomes that undergird the expeditionary narrative—the Missouri and Columbia Basins and the Rocky Mountains—would be welcome.

Similarly, there needs to be a series of ethnological studies like Allen V. Pinkham and Steven R. Evans's *Lewis and Clark among the Nez Perce: Strangers in the Land of the Nimiipuu* (2013). Moving from east to west, the First Nations' stories most in need of telling are the Lakotas, Mandans/Hidatsas, Blackfeet, Shoshones, and Chinooks. The last would be especially desirable because it could help facilitate this tribe's long-overdue procurement of federal recognition. These tribal studies could be nicely complemented with state-based digests of Moulton's *Journals* on the model of Jenkinson's *A Vast and Open Plain: The Writings of the Lewis and Clark Expedition in North Dakota, 1804–1806* (2003) or Robert Carriker and Roger Cooke's *Ocian in View! O! The Joy: Lewis and Clark in Washington State* (2005).

Examinations of trail segments always draw local interest, though more are needed that reach the level of insight and production values found in Rex Ziak's *In Full View* (2002), his study of the expedition on the lower Columbia River. More generally, what we now require, given the standardization of the narrative because of the authoritative nature of the Moulton edition of the journals, is a careful reading of texts to learn more about what they say, not in broad narrative terms, but in their particularity, and also what they do *not* say. All students of Lewis and Clark know the main story lines, so these do not need to be continually rehashed. For instance, the murder/suicide debate would seem to be a good candidate for an interpretive cease-fire. At this point it should only be reopened with new sources, such as what might turn up in Spanish archives. For the field to grow, if not survive, it especially needs to transcend microanalyses of topics that were of purely quotidian interest to Lewis and Clark themselves. For example, the only aspect of the armaments that mattered to the captains was whether they worked or not. How the expedition was outfitted (uniforms, utensils, etc.) is of obvious value to reenactors, and much good research has been done on that topic, but a focus on such ordinary concerns risks trivializing the story and losing potential audiences.

More focus should be lent to the concerns that truly dominated the thinking of Lewis and Clark: (1) achieving the mission of reaching the Pacific; (2) the party's safe return in order to tell their tale; and (3) how their story would come across on the printed page when people like Jefferson, Joseph Banks, or Mackenzie read it. In many respects, an eighteenth- or nineteenth-century expedition never happened unless it was described and explained in book form. Thus discovery as literature is as important a consideration as is discovery as geography. For this reason, Lewis and Clark as travel literature must continue to be studied in comparative context.

An excellent example of this genre is Richard A. Van Orman's *The Explorers: Nineteenth-Century Expeditions in Africa and the American West* (1984), but much remains to be done. Captain Cook's three voyages between the years 1769 and 1780 completed the centuries-long work (inaugurated by Columbus and his peers) of delineating continental outlines below the polar circles. Post-Cook, the discovery impulse in Western civilization shifted to mainland interiors, specifically the sources of rivers—concourses that were the only economical and safe means of access to remote hinterlands. This was the phase of global exploration of which Lewis and Clark were a part, and in one sense Jefferson's instructions to

Lewis can be read as a function of the river source–hunting excitement that began late in the eighteenth century and lasted for much of the nineteenth. Indeed, it might be argued that Jefferson's guidance in this regard misdirected Lewis and Clark. Finding the source of the Missouri on the outbound journey seemed in Lewis's mind (certainly in his journal) to take primacy over discovering a practicable route that might become the Northwest Passage, their ostensible mission. Lewis realized this after the fact, which is why on the return voyage he ran a line from Travelers' Rest to the Great Falls of the Missouri.

The evolution of discovery goals is perhaps best told by the story of John Ledyard, a native of Connecticut whose start in the exploration business came from sailing as a Royal Marine on Cook's third voyage, a venture that was organized just as the American Revolution commenced. After publishing his account of that expedition in 1783, Ledyard tried to organize a fur-trading expedition to the Northwest Coast among his countrymen. His was an attempt at replicating the kind of enterprise that was springing up concurrently within British trading circles in East Asia and Great Britain proper. The most famous of these was the voyage of John Meares, discussed earlier in this book. American businessmen in New England, New York, and Philadelphia were intrigued by Ledyard's proposition, but he was never able to secure their support for his venture. (Had he succeeded, Ledyard would have put together a company prior to the one that funded Robert Gray's voyage to the Pacific Northwest, which he reached in 1788.) So, in 1785 Ledyard decided to pitch his idea in France, during the course of which he met with John Paul Jones, the first famous American naval commander, and Jefferson, at that time the American ambassador to the French court in Paris.

Jefferson found Ledyard to be a compelling figure. In the wake of his book Ledyard was arguably the most famous American-born explorer up to that point in time. Upon Ledyard's failure at cajoling Jones into a competition with British mercantile interests, Jefferson encouraged him to pursue noncommercial avenues that might advance the work of exploration. Accordingly, over the winter of 1785–86 Ledyard abandoned his original fur-trading plan and substituted in its place a quixotic plan for "walking" around the world. This entailed traveling in coach on postal roads across Europe and Siberia to Kamchatka, where he would link up with Russian maritime fur traders. From his personal experience while traveling with Cook, Ledyard knew that Russian merchants carried their vessels across the North Pacific to the Aleutian Islands and the doorstep of the Alaskan subcontinent that Cook was the first to define cartographically. From there Ledyard imagined traveling with a trader of Russian or British origin to the more temperate latitudes of California. Thereafter he envisioned walking to the Atlantic seaboard by way of Kentucky, at that time the western frontier, and then to either New York or, given Jefferson's encouragement, Virginia tidewater.

Jefferson was so enthusiastic about this scheme that he introduced Ledyard to Lafayette, describing his personal qualities in terms which in some measure prefigured the principal skills he later found in Lewis: initiative and scientific inquisitiveness. Both Jefferson and Lafayette provided underwriting for Ledyard's adventure (as did Banks later). In the event, by way of Siberian post road carriage rides Ledyard made it as far as Yakutsk, 90 percent of the way across Russia from St. Petersburg to Okhotsk, in the fall of 1787, but he never moved another mile toward the Pacific Ocean. Russian officials began to suspect that Ledyard was a spy, or an interloper into their fur trade domains, and he was escorted back to Europe and expelled from the country.

When Ledyard surfaced in London in May 1788 he attached himself to the newest discovery rave—Africa. He joined the Association for Promoting the Discovery of the Interior Parts of Africa, founded by Banks, an organization whose name is probative. Cook was dead, and though the era of long-distance voyaging was not over, in Great Britain the new frontier for future discovery was not yet the Pacific Northwest, but instead another great unknown, the interior of Africa. Indeed, what later became known as the Vancouver expedition was originally slated to foster African discovery. In a sense then, Cook's circumnavigations finished the work of discovering continental coastlines and major island groups, at least in the tropical and temperate zones, and so geographic interest began to shift toward continental interiors. The serial North American expeditions of Mackenzie (1789 and 1793) plus Lewis and Clark's search for a riverine version of the Northwest Passage are emblematic of this transference.

As for Ledyard, his new quest for meaning shifted to finding the headwaters of the Niger River in Africa. His plan called for reaching the continental interior by way of the Nile (whose headwaters were another mystery to Europeans). Once inland, Ledyard planned on taking a Nubian trade caravan across the width of Africa in the direction of the Niger's upper reaches near the most exotic place in the world: Timbuktu. The last letter Ledyard wrote was addressed to Jefferson from Cairo on November

15, 1788, on the eve of his expected venture. Unfortunately, his departure from Cairo for the interior was delayed because of intestinal distress, perhaps dysentery, from which he died on January 10, 1789. It is believed that he accidentally overdosed on an emetic intended to induce vomiting but which burst a blood vessel instead. Ledyard died as probably the most famous explorer who never really discovered anything.

Jefferson learned the details surrounding Ledyard's demise during the ensuing spring from British sources, including London newspapers and that towering authority on all matters dealing with discovery, Banks, whose insights were relayed to Paris by no less a figure than Thomas Paine. British colonial officials in Egypt were documented by Paine as Banks's sources, and Paine himself was certainly a reliable correspondent. Thus, it is odd to note that when Jefferson's mini-biography of Lewis appeared in the Biddle account in 1814 he implied that Ledyard had committed suicide as well. Jefferson could have misremembered how Ledyard died, but a likelier explanation is that Jefferson, seizing upon the murky subtext of a misguided attempt at self-medication, endeavored to give Lewis some company in death, to destigmatize it, and make it less exceptional, more human.

This précis of the Ledyard nexus is merely suggestive of what parallel studies of Lewis and Clark's other approximate contemporaries—Vancouver and Mackenzie principally but also the latter's predecessors in northern terrestrial exploration, Canadian fur traders Samuel Hearne and Peter Pond—might yield. The topical and experiential intersections are numerous and the space here allows merely a title-only catalogue: the origin of Jefferson's "courage undaunted" characterization of Lewis's life (a phrase later inverted by Ambrose[1]); how the untimely death of exploratory heroes dominates their historiography; the origin of tactical gambits such as proceeding unarmed into Native encounters and instead incorporating gestures, trifles, or Native raiment; exploratory disappointment as a causative element in the cessation of journal writing; discernment of the expansive nature of indigenous trade networks; the orchestration of sovereignty rites; the ubiquitous nature of Native people interpreting explorers as heaven-born; place-naming commonalities; cartographic evolution and stylistic norms; lessons on how to read a landscape in order to anticipate physiographic consequences such as swift flowing water; the designation of particular regional zones as being fit for European-American colonization; or the application of the ancient principles of equipoise and counterpoise in the anticipation of geographic problems. In regard to this last phenomenon, a reading of the journals of British/Canadian explorers sheds extensive light on the evolution of interlocking rivers as a latter-day Northwest Passage. More particularly, it helps illuminate the origin of Jefferson's instructions to Lewis regarding the notion of a short portage that bridged the Continental Divide.

In the end, Lewis and Clark were no more successful in finding the latest version of the Northwest Passage than (in order) Hearne, Cook, Vancouver, Pond, or Mackenzie were. Indeed, the textual image of North America conveyed in Biddle's version of their journals was the very negation of a shortcut to the markets of Asia. However, the Northwest Passage was a durable idea. In the post-Napoleonic era the quest reverted to its region of origins pre-Cook—the high latitudes of the Arctic Basin—for which period the emblematic figure was the tragic Sir John Franklin. But the turning point in the Northwest Passage saga came with a technological breakthrough: the age of the steam railroad supplanting the age of sail. The key figure here was Isaac I. Stevens, the inaugural governor of Washington Territory. A former army man, Stevens first travelled to his new realm in 1853 with a commission from Secretary of War Jefferson Davis to examine the potential for a transcontinental railroad line running from Lake Superior, once traced by Pond, to Puget Sound, named after one of Vancouver's lieutenants.

Stevens was very conscious of the fact that he was following in the footsteps of Lewis and Clark. His experience is a reminder that the efforts of other American explorers in the Pacific Northwest, such as Charles Wilkes and John C. Frémont, have yet to be mined in a comparative context for interrelated or overlapping themes and experiences. In short, from Cook at the beginning of this era to Stevens at the end, the Lewis and Clark Expedition is its midpoint and there are many insights to be gleaned flowing backward in time or forward.

Official and popular fascination with the Arctic dissipated after 1860 when captains of industry supplanted captains of ships and built what could not be discovered. In the 1880s the fourth variant of the Northwest Passage—the transcontinental railroads reaching Puget Sound and Burrard Inlet—finally realized the long-wished-for commercial potential of a global shortcut.

But perhaps the greatest contribution Lewis and Clark scholars can make is a full-fledged delineation of the expedition within its Enlightenment roots. Enlightenment values, both cultural and scientific, are now commonly written off by some postmodern intersectional commentators as a time-bound cultural construct of limited use toward the achievement of progressive goals. Jefferson is central to the American portion of the Enlightenment, and thus Lewis and Clark with him, but he was a seriously flawed figure because he owned slaves, one of whom was his concubine. As a consequence we are currently witnessing the Hamiltonization of popular culture. This began with the famous Broadway play about Alexander Hamilton but it has been extended in other forms of popular culture. (One can see application of Hamilton's imagined democratizing ethos to such disparate figures as Winston Churchill and Katherine Graham in the films *Darkest Hour* [2017] and *The Post* [2017]. Here I am thinking of the imaginary scenes where Churchill conducts a demographically idealized focus group about whether to resist Nazi Germany, or when Graham emerges from a Supreme Court hearing and wades through a crowd of acolytes.) The real Hamilton made many contributions to American history, but in the rush to contrast him with an increasingly demonized Jefferson, his monarchial if not Napoleonic tendencies are being overlooked—for example, his role in suppressing the Whiskey Rebellion.

The greater irony is that Enlightenment-era exploration gradually guided Western civilization to an appreciation for the autonomous value of indigenous cultures, which, not coincidentally, at the same time began to exhibit a less exalted view of itself. The Enlightenment was the very origin of the valorization of pluralism and multiculturalism that dominates the avowed sensibility of modern times.

There are related incongruities. The academy and media illuminati are agog over the emergence of the "post truth" era in American politics, but this movement's origins lie not in some reflexive populism but rather the rejection of the very idea of objectivity by postmodern scholars. The foundation for sophisticated understanding of any phenomenon, substantial or ephemeral, is being able to measure it, and Enlightenment science laid down the baseline of data in chemistry, biology, astronomy, and yes, global geography. A lot has been lost in the transit from Cook's contemporary in French Enlightenment discovery, Louis-Antoine de Bougainville, to the founder of postmodern social theory and literary criticism, French philosopher Paul-Michel Foucault. The Enlightenment's perspective in search of broad truths about the cosmos and humanity's place in it has been fractured by the prism of subjectivities into miniaturized academic disciplines, identity politics, and what might be called the rise of tribalized "witness studies." The logic of authoritative competence has shifted from rationalism and a hierarchy of knowledge to the whims of emotive ideologies and personal self-reflection viewed solely through the lens of race and gender.

As for postcolonial and postmodern scholarship, much of it is not history at all but rather moral posturing pretending to be social science. Perhaps its worst excess in relation to the history of discovery is positioning Enlightenment period explorers under the metaphorical tyranny of Kurtz, Joseph Conrad's central character in *Heart of Darkness* (1899). This gothic trope is actually a legacy of the Romantic era whose seedtime came during the unleashing of personal and ideological passions in Revolutionary France and which took a firm hold of Western literary arts in the post-Napoleonic era. Historians have a role to play in helping society to recover from this kind of distortion, but what we truly need today as an antidote to our current epidemic of moral absolutism is an entirely new secular Age of Enlightenment that aims to mitigate the problems of our times by freely crossing intellectual and cultural boundaries, discovering along the way the universality of the human experience. We continue to need such explorers, and to study them, for as T. S. Eliot wrote:

> We shall not cease from exploration
> And the end of all our exploring
> Will be to arrive where we started
> And know the place for the first time.

NOTES

1. See David L. Nicandri, "The Cook Template," *We Proceeded On,* 46:2 (May 2020): 14-21, where I address this topic within a comparison of Cook's instruction from the Admiralty with those Jefferson drafted for Lewis.

SUGGESTED READING

KEY EXPLORATORY JOURNALS

Beaglehole, John C., editor. *The Journals of Captain James Cook on His Voyages of Discovery*. 3 volumes. Cambridge: Cambridge University Press, 1955–67.

Forster, George. *A Voyage Round the World*. Nicholas Thomas and Oliver Berghof, editors. Honolulu: University of Hawaii Press, 2000.

Lamb, W. Kaye, editor. *The Journals and Letters of Sir Alexander Mackenzie*. London: Cambridge University Press, 1970.

Moulton, Gary E., editor. *The Journals of the Lewis & Clark Expedition*. 13 volumes. Lincoln: University of Nebraska Press, 1983–2001.

Vancouver, George. *A Voyage of Discovery to the North Pacific Ocean and Round the World, 1791–1795*. W. Kaye Lamb, editor. 4 volumes. London: Hakluyt Society, 1984.

SECONDARY ACCOUNTS

Allen, John Logan. *Lewis and Clark and the Image of the American Northwest*. Reprint edition. New York: Dover, 1991.

Ambrose, Stephen. *Undaunted Courage: Meriwether Lewis, Thomas Jefferson, and the Opening of the American West*. New York: Simon & Schuster, 1996.

Beckham, Stephen Dow. *Lewis and Clark: From the Rockies to the Pacific*. Portland, OR: Graphics Arts Center Publishing, 2002.

Beckham, Stephen Dow et al. *The Literature of the Lewis and Clark Expedition: A Bibliography and Essays*. Portland, OR: Lewis & Clark College, 2003.

Botkin, Daniel. *Beyond the Stony Mountains: Nature in the American West from Lewis and Clark to Today*. Oxford: Oxford University Press, 2004.

_____. *Our Natural History: The Lessons of Lewis and Clark*. New York: G. P. Putnam's Sons, 1995.

Carriker, Robert C., and Roger Cooke. *Ocian in View! O! The Joy: Lewis and Clark in Washington State*. Tacoma: Washington State Historical Society, 2005.

Danisi, Thomas C. *Uncovering the Truth About Meriwether Lewis*. Amherst, NY: Prometheus Books, 2012.

Danisi, Thomas C., and John C. Jackson. *Meriwether Lewis*. Amherst, NY: Prometheus Books, 2009.

Duncan, Dayton. *Out West: A Journey Through Lewis and Clark's America*. Reprint edition. Lincoln: University of Nebraska Press, 2000.

Furtwangler, Albert. *Acts of Discovery: Visions of America in the Lewis and Clark Journals*. Urbana: University of Illinois Press, 1993.

Gilman, Carolyn Ives. *Lewis and Clark: Across the Divide*. Washington, DC: Smithsonian Institution Press, 2003.

Goetzmann, William H. *New Lands, New Men: America and the Second Great Age of Discovery*. New York: Viking, 1986.

Gough, Barry. *First across the Continent: Sir Alexander Mackenzie*. Norman: University of Oklahoma Press, 1997.

Hayes, Derek. *First Crossing: Alexander Mackenzie, His Expedition across North America, and the Opening of the Continent.* Seattle: Sasquatch Books, 2001.

Holmberg, James J., editor. *Dear Brother: Letters of William Clark to Jonathan Clark.* New Haven, CT: Yale University Press, 2002.

Horwitz, Tony. *Blue Latitudes: Boldly Going Where Captain Cook Has Gone Before.* New York: Picador/Henry Holt, 2002.

Jenkinson, Clay. *The Character of Meriwether Lewis: "Completely Metamorphosed" in the American West.* Reno, NV: Marmarth Press, 2000.

_____. *A Vast and Open Plain: The Writings of the Lewis and Clark Expedition in North Dakota, 1804–1806.* Bismarck: State Historical Society of North Dakota, 2003.

_____. *The Character of Meriwether Lewis: Explorer in the Wilderness.* Bismarck, ND: Dakota Institute Press, 2011.

McLynn, Frank. *Captain Cook: Master of the Seas.* New Haven, CT: Yale University Press, 2011.

Nicandri, David L. *River of Promise: Lewis and Clark on the Columbia.* Bismarck, ND: Dakota Institute Press, 2009.

Nokes, J. Richard. *Almost a Hero: The Voyages of John Meares, R. N., to China, Hawaii, and the Northwest Coast.* Pullman: Washington State University Press, 1998.

Philbrick, Nathaniel. *Sea of Glory: America's Voyage of Discovery, The U.S. Exploring Expedition, 1838–1842.* New York: Viking, 2003.

Pinkham, Allen, and Steven R. Evans. *Lewis and Clark among the Nez Perce: Strangers in the Land of the Nimiipuu.* Bismarck, ND: Dakota Institute Press, 2013.

Plamondon II, Martin. *Lewis and Clark Trail Maps: A Cartographic Reconstruction.* 3 volumes. Pullman: Washington State University Press, 2000–4.

Ronda, James. P. *Lewis and Clark among the Indians.* Lincoln: University of Nebraska Press, 1984.

_____. *Voyages of Discovery: Essays on the Lewis and Clark Expedition.* Helena: Montana Historical Society Press, 1998.

Slaughter, Thomas P. *Exploring Lewis and Clark: Reflections on Men and Wilderness.* New York: Alfred A. Knopf, 2003.

Smith, Bernard. *European Vision and the South Pacific.* 2nd Edition. New Haven, CT: Yale University Press, 1985.

_____. *Imagining the Pacific: In the Wake of the Cook Voyages.* New Haven, CT: Yale University Press, 1992.

Van Orman, Richard A. *The Explorers: Nineteenth-Century Expeditions in Africa and the American West.* Albuquerque: University of New Mexico Press, 1984.

Wood, W. Raymond. *Prologue to Lewis and Clark: The Mackay and Evans Expedition.* Norman: University of Oklahoma Press, 2003.

Ziak, Rex. *In Full View: A True and Accurate Account of Lewis and Clark's Arrival at the Pacific Ocean, and Their Search for a Winter Camp along the Lower Columbia River.* Astoria, OR: Moffitt House Press, 2002.

CREDITS

THE FOLLOWING CHAPTERS APPEARED IN THEIR ORIGINAL FORM AS:

Chapter 1: "Lewis and Clark in the Age of Cook: An Essay on Enlightenment Exploration," *We Proceeded On* 39: 4 (November 2013): 15–23.

Chapter 2: "Lewis and Clark: Exploring under the Influence of Alexander Mackenzie," *Pacific Northwest Quarterly* 95: 4 (Fall 2004): 171–81.

Chapter 3: "The Rhyme of the Great Navigator: The Literature of Captain Cook and Its Influence on the Journals of Lewis and Clark—Part 1, A Canoe's Teeth," *We Proceeded On* 42: 1 (February 2016): 22–28; "Part 2, The Grandest Sight," 42: 2 (May 2016): 17–23; "Part 3, This Sublunary World," 42: 3 (August 2016): 24–27.

Chapter 5: "The Illusion of Cape Disappointment," *We Proceeded On* 30: 4 (November 2004): 15–21.

Chapter 6: "Meriwether Lewis: The Solitary Hero," *We Proceeded On* 35: 4 (November 2009): 8–15.

Chapter 7: "Pure Water: Meriwether Lewis's Homesickness at Fort Clatsop," *We Proceeded On* 43: 3 (August 2017): 10–17.

Epilogue: "The Study of Lewis and Clark: Where We Are Now and Where We Ought to Go Next," *We Proceeded On* 44: 3 (August 2018): 5–9.

About the Author

David L. Nicandri directed the Washington State Historical Society from 1987 to 2011, during which time he also edited *Columbia Magazine*. Prior to that role, he held the position of historian at the Washington State Capital Museum from 1972 to 1987. His publications include *River of Promise: Lewis and Clark on the Columbia*, and *Captain Cook Rediscovered: Voyaging in the Icy Latitudes*. He is currently working on a monograph tentatively entitled, "Discovering Nothing: The Evolution of the Pacific Portal to the Northwest Passage," a sequel to *Captain Cook Rediscovered*. He holds honorary doctorates from Gonzaga University, the University of Puget Sound, and the University of Idaho, and currently serves on the Board of Trustees for The Evergreen State College.

INDEX

Thwaites, Reuben Gold, 79–81
Tongue Point, 81
transcontinental railroad, 140. *See also* Isaac
   I. Stevens
Transit of Venus, 7, 48, 127. *See also* Cook,
   1ˢᵗ voyage
Traveler's Rest, 100n21, 137
Tuchman, Barbara, 12
Twisted Hair, 22. *See also* Lewis and Clark,
   Native guides and Nez Perce Indians

United States, American Indian policy, 125;
   Army, 122; commercial policy, 32–33;
   competition with British interests,
   32–33; Congress, 114, 123–25,
   128; Constitution, 124; Exploring
   Expedition (1838–1842); *See* Wilkes,
   expedition); Navy, 122, 124–25, 127;
   Revolutionary War, 13, 122, 137;
   sovereignty, 121; Supreme Court, 141;
   territorial claims, 121–22, 124–25; War
   of 1812, 114, 122

Valdés, Cayetano, 2, 4
Van Buren, Martin, 126–7
Van Orman, Richard A., 39, 136
Vancouver Island, 9, 30, 87n27; Mackenzie's
   arrival near, 43; Spanish exploration
   of, 2
Vancouver, George, 9, 20, 139; account of
   Pacific explorations, 76–77; British
   delegate to Spanish at Nootka, 4, 44;
   cartography, 6, 34n14, 87n27; on the
   Columbia, 76, 82, 84–85, 87n27; on
   Cook's 2ⁿᵈ voyage, 48; criticism from
   Clark, 84; expedition, 4, 37–38, 86n18,
   123, 138, 140, influence on Clark,
   85; influence of Cook, 44; influence
   on Jefferson, 77; influence on Lewis,
   34n14, 84; influence on Lewis and
   Clark Expedition, 6, 34n14, 37–38,
   85, 133; influence on Mackenzie, 17;
   influence of Meares, 44; influence of
   Wales, 48; legacy, 1; naming of places,
   121; negotiation with Spain at Nootka
   Sound, 4; at the Northwest Coast, 4,
   123; official account of voyage, 116; in
   the Pacific, 37, 123; at Puget Sound,
   121, 140; search for Northwest Passage,
   11, 17, 37–38, 45, 77, 123, 126, 140;
   and Vancouver Island, 9. *See also* Cook,
   2ⁿᵈ voyage

Virginia, 12, 107, 114, 116, 118, 129, 138

Wahkiakum Indian village, 83
Wales, William, 37, 48, 51–54. *See also* Cook,
   2ⁿᵈ voyage
War of 1812, 114, 122
Warfington, Richard, 72–73
Washington, 16, 79–80, 82–83, 121, 140.
Washington D.C., 38, 107, 115, 118, 125
Washington, George, 122
Weippe Prairie, 28
Weiser, Peter, 67. *See also* Lewis and Clark,
   crew
Whiskey Rebellion, 113, 141
White Cliffs, 80
White Earth Creek, 69
White House, 107, 114.
Whitehouse, Joseph, 70–71, 73; influence
   of Alexander Mackenzie, 31; journal,
   30–31, 35n50, 61–62, 70–72, 80, 85,
   87n28, 89; plagiarism of Mackenzie,
   31. *See also* Lewis and Clark, crew
"Whitehouse's Creek," 70
White River, 66
Wilkes, Charles, 113, 121, 140; appointment
   as commander of US Exploring
   Expedition, 127–29; on the Columbia,
   121; comparisons to Clark, 128;
   comparisons to Cook, 127; dispute
   with Dickerson, 126–27; dog, 129; in
   England, 126–7; expedition, 121–23,
   125, 127–130, 140; historiography,
   122; influence of Cook, 121; influence
   of Dickerson, 113; influence of Lewis,
   129; influence of Mackenzie, 129;
   influence of Malaspina, 121; influence
   of La Pérouse, 121. *See also* United
   States, Exploring Expedition (1838–
   1842)
Willard, Alexander, 62, 89–90
Windsor, Richard, 67. *See also* Lewis and
   Clark, crew
Wisdom (tributary of the Jefferson River),
   72, 97
Wistar, Caspar, 115
Wood River, 85n, 93

Yellowstone River, 4, 20, 66, 94, 98
York, 16, 134. *See also* Lewis and Clark, crew
Young, Edward, 55–57

Ziak, Rex, 19, 79–80, 102, 136